# Caucasus

*Also by Nicholas Griffin*

The Requiem Shark
The House of Sight and Shadow

# Caucasus

*A Journey to the Land between Christianity and Islam*

NICHOLAS GRIFFIN

The University of Chicago Press

# For TJD

The University of Chicago Press, Chicago, 60637
Copyright © 2001 by Nicholas Griffin
All rights reserved. Published by arrangement with Thomas Dunne Books,
an imprint of St. Martin's Press, LLC
First published in Great Britain by Review, an imprint of Headline Book Publishing
Published in the United States by St. Martin's Press, 2003
University of Chicago Press edition 2004

Printed in the United States of America
10 09 08 07 06 05 04     1 2 3 4 5

ISBN: 0-226-30859-6 (paperback)

Photographs of "Ancient watchtowers in northern Georgia," "Car and occupants,"
"Hinaliq," "Bandiev Kishi with evidence of his great age," and "The team"
all © John Boit.

Library of Congress Cataloging-in-Publication Data

Griffin, Nicholas, 1971–
    Caucasus : a journey to the land between Christianity and Islam /
Nicholas Griffin.
        p.    cm.
    Originally published: 1st U.S. ed. New York : St. Martin's, 2003.
    Includes bibliographical references and index.
    ISBN 0-226-30859-6 (pbk. : alk. paper)
        1. Caucasus—Description and travel.   2. Shâmil, Imâm, 1798?–1871.
    3. Griffin, Nicholas, 1971—Travel—Caucasus.   I. Title.

    DK509 .G74 2004
    947.5′086—dc22
                                                    2003063352

The paper used in this publication meets the minimum requirements of the
American National Standard for Information Sciences-Permanence of Paper for
Printed Library Materials, ANSI Z39.48-1992.

# Contents

*Illustrations follow page 52.*

# Acknowledgements and Thanks

Above all: to my travelling companions, John Boit, Ilya Suleymanov and Taran Davies.

Outside the Caucasus: to Irina Prentice and to her grandmother, Irina Bergmann, and their friend Marc Alexander. To Emilia Sherifova and her family; Marilyn Perry of the World Monuments Fund; John Richardson, formerly of Iridium; Bartle Bull; John Bruno of the Explorers' Club. To Garo Keheyan and Sasha Abercorn for invaluable contacts.

In Azerbaijan: special thanks are owed to our two hosts, Dr Tim Bentley and George Noel-Clarke, who showed extraordinary patience to suffer through our comings and goings. Our trip could not have been the same without the help of Vahid Mustafayev and his company, Azerbaijan News Service (ANS). Not only did he provide us with our friend and driver Ramiz Norbalayev, but he also constantly surprised us with the lengths to which he would go to aid us. Many thanks to Vafa Guluzade for taking the time to meet us. Also to Kay Burn Lim, Don Churchman, Bill Reynolds, Jim Philipov, Rena Effendi, Professor Yaqub Mahmudlu, Zhura and Said, Ali Asaev and Fatima Aslan. To the Ambassador Stanley T. Escudero and his son, Alex Escudero; to Azad Dashdamirov, Fuad Akhundov and Suad Fataliyev.

In Armenia: many thanks to Ararat Sargsyan, his son Arshak

and to his entire family, who treated us as their own during our stay in Armenia. There have never been better hosts. And thanks to their friends who showed great patience and warmth: Hovik Kochinian, Samvel Mkrtichian, Vartan Garoyan, Nazaret, Marina and Nare Karoyan, Marcos Grigorian and Saak Pogosyan. Also to Vartan Oskanian for taking the time to meet with us.

In Karabagh: thanks to Naira Melkoumian, Minister of Foreign Affairs.

In Georgia: special thanks are due to Marika Didebulidze, who went far beyond the call of duty in assisting us. Also to the Fund for the Preservation of Cultural Heritage of Georgia and to David Ninidze, Khaka Khimshiashvili, Yorgi Otkumezuri and Nino Bagrationi. To Irakli and Ketevan Sutidze, the finest of artists. To Professor Gocha Khundadze and Professor Mikhail Samsauadze of Tbilisi State University. For their openness and kindness, thanks to Gela Charkviani, Adviser to the President, and to Mamuka Areshidze, Head of the Commission on the relations with the People of Caucasia. To Vasha and Marina Chincharauli in Shateli. And warmest thanks to both Tamara Shamil and Merab Kokoshashvili who spoke so openly of their family histories.

Books: though a full bibliography is given elsewhere in *Caucasus*, I wish to acknowledge a special debt to Baddeley, Blanch and Lieven.

The city formerly known as Tiflis is always referred to by its modern name, Tbilisi.

# Foreword

Our journey to the Caucasus brought no definitive reward. We went in search of a legend and found it sometimes burnished, sometimes burning bright. We were trying to measure the effect one man can have on his region's history 150 years after his death. This figure, Shamil, was an Islamic mountain warrior leading diverse tribes against Russia. But in what way is a legend passed through generations? Why is he evoked, and when? Does anything of a man remain once he has become a myth?

These were all cloudy questions; and yet, during our journey in the summer of 1999, everything was suddenly jolted into focus. We had gone sniffing after a trail of bloodshed as old as man, and found ourselves witnessing the prelude of yet another round in one of the longest on-going conflicts in the world – Russia against the mountains of the Caucasus. The past and the present, no matter how divergent they seemed at the beginning of our journey, were slowly being stitched together again. This, to me, is the effect of the Caucasus. I am not suggesting that the echo of history in the early twenty-first century is so precise that nineteenth-century differences have been erased, but the reverberations are considerable. I hope they justify covering old ground, if only to compare it to the new.

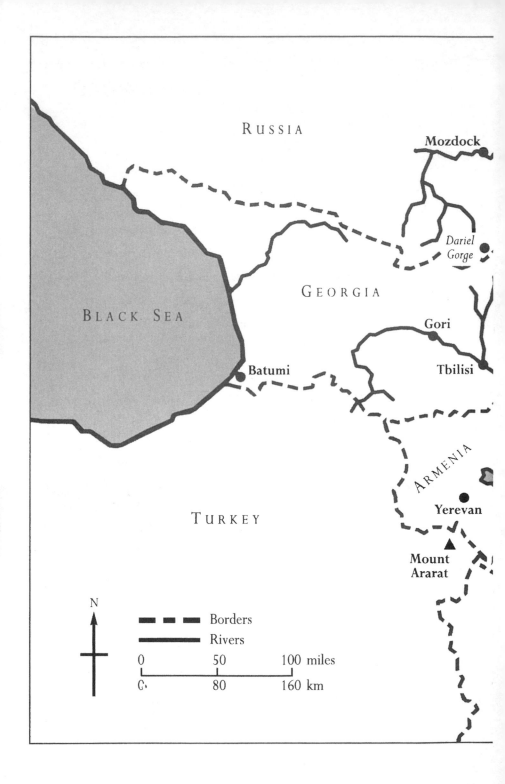

RUSSIA

Mozdock

*Dariel Gorge*

GEORGIA

BLACK SEA

Gori

Batumi

Tbilisi

ARMENIA

Yerevan

TURKEY

Mount Ararat

N

Borders
Rivers

| 0 | 50 | 100 miles |
| 0 | 80 | 160 km |

# CHAPTER 1

# Jagged Land

*The Caucasus is a jagged land. Imagine powerful neighbours: Iran to the south, Russia to the north, Turkey to the west, hemmed by the Black Sea on one side and the Caspian Sea on the other. If the Caucasus didn't already possess the highest mountain range in Europe, the political pressure exerted from all sides would have forced the land to crack and rise. Now elect a conqueror. Genghis Khan, Alexander the Great, Tamerlane, a caravan of Persian kings, Peter the Great, Hitler, Stalin have all claimed conquest of the Caucasus. Choose a religion. Shiite Muslims to the south, Sunnis to the north; three schisms of Christianity push from separate fronts.*

To attempt to unravel the history of the Caucasus would force the presumption that history would cease moving long enough for a considered look. Perhaps this would have been possible if the most recent conqueror of the region had been anyone but the Soviet Union, and though the Soviets were kind enough to leave behind enough power lines and vodka to keep people drinking deep into the night, they were not so direct with the histories of their satellite states. Soviet Russia did not hesitate to rewrite history, not just once, but repeatedly.

Even before the Soviets this was a land of myths and tales as tall as the peaks themselves. 'All Caucasians are great liars,' said one of our hosts in the three competing countries of Transcaucasia. In Armenia, Noah's Ark lies on the borders. In Azerbaijan, the Garden of Eden is said to lurk somewhere in the south. Georgia is not to be outdone. If her neighbours boast of the genesis of man, Georgia claims to have been home to the gods. Prometheus was bound to one of her great peaks, his liver torn daily by the circling birds of prey.

Everything shifts in the Caucasus, blown by some of the strongest winds on earth. Even the ground moves, splintered by fault lines. In early Georgian myths, it is said that when the mountains were young, they had legs – could walk from the edges of the oceans to the deserts, flirting with the low hills, shrouding them with soft clouds of love. History, of course, is the greatest shape-changer of them all. The further back you peer into the stories of the Caucasus, the more likely you are to be confounded by webs of contradiction and myth.

Head north in the Caucasus and the hordes of languages will confuse you. Imagine walking around the Eiffel Tower on a busy summer's day and hearing the sounds of dozens of nationalities. Now imagine that no one has travelled more than fifty miles to get there. This is the problem: everybody is more or less at home and everybody is more or less in some kind of conflict. Not necessarily bloody, but often political, often territorial.

According to Brzezinski, America's former National Security Adviser, there is no more important area in the world than the

Caucasus. Geopolitically, it is the pivot about which everything sways: American economic interests, Russian territorial interests, Islamic religious interests, all factors in the oscillating local politics. It was considered just as critical 150 years ago, a narrow but vital bridge.

The Caucasus Mountains form a natural border to the Russian empire. By 1859, at the end of a war conducted throughout the Caucasus, Russia's influence only stopped at the Persian court. Some 140 years later, the tide of Russian empire was receding with the fall of the Soviet system, once again pausing at the foot of the mountains. In the summer of 1999, Boris Yeltsin, then President of Russia, made a statement: 'The single biggest problem facing Russia today is Chechnya.' Leading his country to a humiliating withdrawal from Chechen soil in 1996 had not affected Russia's phantom pains of the lost empire. The Caucasus was the testing ground for Russian strength as she expanded. It is also proving to be the testing ground of her strength as she contracts. One thing cannot be changed: Russia borders the Caucasus. No one can move mountains.

What was, what is, everybody after? Influence, power, land, of course. But what brings the lands of the Caucasus above simpler questions of nationalism and self-determination is oil. There is an estimated 100 billion barrels of crude oil in the Caspian Sea, great quantities of which belong to Azerbaijan, which, like its neighbours Georgia and Armenia, has been independent of Russia since 1991. Russia is not resigned to seeing this potential source of revenue go.

I am heading to the Caucasus to trace the legacy of one of its greatest heroes. Not the most famous – that would be the Georgian Stalin – but Imam Shamil, a figure revered throughout the region, yet virtually unknown to the West. It wasn't always so. Immediately preceding Britain's involvement in the Crimean War the Imam (a Muslim term for a religious and political leader) was a front-page regular of the London *Times*. By the time Britain went to war with the Tsar in 1854, Shamil had been fighting against the Russians for over twenty years, desperately trying to maintain the independence of the Caucasus Mountains. The land he defended was both minuscule and thinly populated when compared with Russia. In the London newspapers, Shamil was presented as a noble savage, a literary creation guaranteed to appeal to both sexes. Sitting astride his horse, black banners and beard blowing in the mountain gales, he was depicted as a man of impeccable honour resisting the greedy southern push of Russia. Tales were reported with suitable exaggeration. Shamil, it was said, often fought the Russians alone, beheading the opposing cavalry, leaping chasms and plunging off cliffs to escape. *The Times* interpreted Russian movement in the Caucasus as a threat to India, Britain's prize possession. Lose India and Queen Victoria would never become an empress.

Accordingly, the figure of Shamil was raised to the British public as a paragon of resistance. They imbued him with what the Victorian era had decided were British virtues: endurance, intelligence and a natural nobility. So often did Shamil appear in *The Times* that copies of the newspaper finally ended up in his own hands, thousands of miles from London, in the airy crags of southern Dagestan, ten thousand feet above the sea.

Shamil may have found some truth in the newspapers interpreted for him. It was true he fought against the Russians, true he was vastly outnumbered, true he had endured year after year through tremendous displays of tactical ability. Yet he was not so insulated to ignore the certainty that his resistance would eventually falter without outside assistance. This prompted him to address Her Majesty Queen Victoria:

For years, O honoured Queen, we have been at war against Russia, our invader. Every year we must defend ourselves against the invader's fresh armies which pour into our valleys. Our resistance is stubborn, altogether we are obliged, in winter, to send our wives and children far away, to seek safety in the forests, where they have nothing, no food, no refuge against the severe cold. Yet we are resigned. It is Allah's will. He ordained that we should suffer to defend our land. But England must know of this – of our cease-less struggle against Russia . . . We beseech you, we urge you, O Queen, to bring us aid.[1]

The Queen had already responded favourably to similar causes of independence. Garibaldi had been well treated on a visit to London just the year before, appreciated by all classes of society. Her Majesty was moved to order a report on the matter of Shamil. He had become Britain's hero of the hour. Large demonstrations gathered in Birmingham, heralding the resistance of the 'Lion of Dagestan'. What particularly concerned the Midlands also concerned the British Government, namely their cotton manufacturing being affected by a Russian presence so close to India. The Foreign Office eyed Shamil coldly, but the British press was busy stoking its own fires. *The Times* cried, 'Let the English resolutely declare themselves the generous defenders of liberty, and their moral influence will overwhelm the brutal forces of the Russian Empire.'

The Government refused to act. Britain, after all, had much more in common with invaders, rather than the invaded. While foreign policy remained frozen, sixty volunteer freedom fighters headed for the Caucasus. Sir Richard Burton was supposed to lead an expedition in aid of Shamil, but the idea was soon aborted. Guns were run across the Black Sea, but Shamil was looking for more than a gossamer gesture of support. Without outside assistance, the fight would always remain one of resistance. The mythical figure of the Imam conjured by the English press was to continue to fight, but condemned to fight alone.

# CHAPTER 2

# Based in Baku

*Today, the group who has come in search of Shamil's legacy has gathered in Baku. Beside me, in a lolling taxi with sharp springs, is John Boit, a gravel-voiced photographer from Maine. He is an outdoors man, a fisherman and a reporter who earns his living among the newspapers of Azerbaijan and by taking photographs for the premier American newspapers. It is John's voice that holds the attention, not the shaved head, not the beginnings of a goatee or the calmest blue eyes. His voice is a most versatile instrument. Between the airport and the city he is already bending it into exact impressions and caricatures.*

Taran sits smoking in the front seat. His video camera is on his lap. He runs his hand through his long brown hair. It is unbearably hot, but Taran has directed films in the deserts of Central Asia and on the shores of Lake Baikal. The wind takes the ash from his cigarette, leaving the tip glowing with heat. Taran and I have known each other for half our lives. He told me of Shamil, of the film he wanted to make about the echoes of one man's life. Would I like to help dig for the half buried, for the traces of a man's effect a century and a half later?

Sitting on my other side is Ilya Suleymanov, an Uzbek Jew whom Taran met just south of the Karakum Desert while making his last film. A year later, Ilya turned up on Taran's doorstep in New York, six thousand miles from his native sands and cities. He already knows all about America, has been to Yankee Stadium, and around the five boroughs working in his limousine. Taran calls him the 'facilitator'. Ilya is also our translator, which is odd, since he speaks little English.

Earlier today, flying to Baku, I met Ilya for the first time. He came to sit beside me on the empty aeroplane. Uncomfortable, he brought his feet on to the seat and assumed a squat: feet flat, rear end suspended between his shins.

'Cat's legs look like carrot,' said Ilya.

'Excuse me?'

'Seven, twenty-four,' he said, nodding his head, 'cats no got fat feet.'

'I have no idea what you're talking about,' I explained.

Ilya banged the back of the seat in front of him and laughed. 'My English. Fucked up. One hundred precent.'

For a moment Ilya disappeared, then jumped back into his seat, resuming his position with two small vodkas and two bottles of wine. They were offered to me. He poured one vodka and one wine into the same glass, mixed it with his finger and downed it, then repeated the process.

Taran was lying across from us, asleep. I closed my eyes in imitation of the director and when I opened them five minutes later, Ilya was gone. He didn't reappear until the very end of the flight when the plane descended with an ominous thump and veered across the runway. Overhead compartments popped open, as did the door to the bathroom and Ilya lurched down the aisle towards us, buckling his belt. We were still travelling at well over a hundred miles an hour. A flight attendant shouted from his seat: 'Sir, sir, sit down, sir' Ilya paused and looked up, confused. 'You must sit down,' continued the flight attendant. 'You're endangering the lives of other passengers.'

Ilya cackled.

'Sit down,' screamed the flight attendant.

Everybody turned to see Ilya. 'You,' he shouted back to the attendant. 'I fucking *kill* you.' The flight attendant sat down first, then Ilya collapsed in his seat.

'You're drunk,' accused Taran.

'Not drunk,' slurred Ilya, 'sleeping.'

This was how we had entered Baku, our gateway to the Caucasus. In the late nineteenth century, after Russia had annexed the entire region, the Caspian was the centre of the world's oil production and if the Caspian had had a capital, there is no doubt that it would have been Baku. Sometime boomtown, it began the twentieth century as the world's number-one producer of oil and ended it as a source of massive potential, drawing all of the world's oil companies to the shores of the Caspian.

Baku, now the capital of the Republic of Azerbaijan, is still a city set on the edge of wealth. It remains the richest city of the Caucasus, not a poor choice for a starting point to edge towards the mountains. You can look out from its harbour and see oil platforms rising lazily from the sea, common as shorebirds. Baku is supposed to be the city of winds, the Chicago of the Caspian, but gusts are not constant. Summer lulls of heavy humidity are broken by strong winds that sweep into the park-lined promenades, rattling swarms of discarded sunflower seeds along the streets. The wind blows through the Old City, a hive of narrow streets defended on three sides by a crenellated wall, then along avenues of stone mansions raised at the height of Baku's oil wealth. As the winds gust they reach the concrete suburbs, Soviet monoliths scattered with no seeming purpose other than to scar the landscape. Abruptly, the suburbs are followed by empty, arid land.

Baku's coast is a mixture of yellow sands and black oils. Nodding derricks gather like packs of donkeys in the oilfields. Up and down, up and down, heads shaking in perpetual agreement. Or rather they would nod if more than the odd one was working. With foreign investment came embassy staffs and oilmen who form the main body of the two thousand overseas workers in Baku. A man known as Doctor Tim has agreed to put us up. He lives away from the centre of town, away from the expatriates. At thirtysomething, Doctor Tim is an expat whose magazine good looks and well-cut suits are distinctly at odds with the dust and rubble of his neighbourhood, in which palatial oil houses rub shoulders with rundown shacks. There are pot-holes around that could double as trenches. After a few months in the gold mines of Tajikistan, the Doctor moved to Baku as a physician dealing almost exclusively with expatriates. Like so many, he now harbours schemes, projects and dreams of fortune.

'No problems with water here,' says the Doctor from the front porch of his walled and whitewashed home. 'We're on the same pipe as the President's house. Electricity, too.'

Doctor Tim is imparting the dos and don'ts of Baku, as we all stand around him, cradling cooling pinch glasses of tea. 'When the police stop you,' he says, 'just don't get out of the car. When they ask for your passport, don't give it to them. You've done nothing wrong, let them rant, they'll get bored. If you're really worried, get a cell phone and your embassy's number.'

'Why would they stop us?'

'Because you're here.'

An hour later, Doctor Tim tires of drinking tea. We lock the gate to his house, squeeze into a taxi and head towards an expatriate bar called Adam's Diner. Ilya stares at the streets we pass through, letting Doctor Tim and John carry the conversation. The buildings are soaked in grubby pollution, a pronounced air of yesteryear. I wonder where Ilya's mind has drifted to. Yesterday he had talked briefly of his first trip to Baku, a dozen years ago, to visit his uncle. Everything, he insisted, had changed beyond recognition, but nothing had shocked him more than the condition of the people. He had already found professors as taxi drivers, an Interpol agent moonlighting as a tour guide. But that afternoon Ilya's mood had lightened. I had seen him playing in the street with a gang of young boys, picking one up, swirling him around, delighting them all. Even the street curs had been petted and pampered.

Taran is also wrapped in silence. Occasionally he pinches his lip, lost in thought. Despite years of friendship, I realize that, thousands of miles from home, I have no idea what he is thinking. He has, to some extent, isolated himself from the rest of the group. Perhaps he is pondering his responsibilities, perhaps he is thinking only of his film, his eyes just an extended lens of his camera.

Adam's Diner is an odd place to begin the search for the legacy of Imam Shamil. It seems the further expatriates live from home the more familiar they like their environments. Adam's has dark wooden floors, red checked tablecloths, staff dressed in pressed white shirts and black trousers. We could be in any one of a thousand cities. At the bar is a Scotsman called Neil Wilson, celebrating his last night in Azerbaijan. He's heavily tanned, affable and extremely happy to be heading back to Edinburgh. He works for Lonely Planet and has spent the last six weeks scouring every dust-choked road and rocky outcrop for his forthcoming guide-book.

'How long are you here for?' he asks.

'Two months, maybe three.'

He shakes his head and laughs. 'There's nothing here. Nothing. Some impressive mountains, but apart from that, it's going to be a long summer.'

'There's one guidebook already, isn't there?' I ask.

'Thank God,' said Neil. 'Very useful. Paved the way, if you like. Poor man was arrested, oh, say, six times. You know how it is, wandering around small towns, scribbling notes. They're all used to the Soviet times, presume on you being a spy. In for question-ing, spend the night . . .' Neil leans over. 'Pretty much depends on where you're going, though.'

'North,' I answer. 'See how close we can get to Chechnya and Dagestan.'

'You'd better be insured then.'

'For kidnapping?'

He nods. 'There's not much in the way of borders up there, they come across, take you, drag you back. Had a video on TV the other day of some Chechens sawing off the finger of a mission-ary. They sent it to his family.'

We sip our beers. 'We're covered for five million dollars,' I confess.

'That's fantastic,' says Neil, 'you should tell everybody. Or maybe just put a dollar sign on your head.' He smiles. 'Keep it quiet. You never know who you're talking to.'

Ilya is celebrating in his own manner, drinking beer, circling the bar with one eye on a silent television, the other scanning female figures. By one the bar is emptying, we pile into a taxi, our host, Doctor Tim, in the front seat, and set off on the short drive.

As we slowly swing through a roundabout, Ilya rolls down a window. We pull level at a red light with a police car, crowded with large silhouettes.

Ilya leans out of the window, neck craning towards the police, and shouts at the top of his lungs. What he says nobody knows, but the reaction is certain. On goes the siren of the police car and they accelerate past our taxi, then brake sharply. All four leap out and surround the vehicle.

'What did you say?' asks Doctor Tim.

'I just tell them hallo.' Ilya laughs. 'Don't worry, I take care of it.'

'We're going to have the crap beaten out of us,' says the Doctor.

'I thought we just stay in the car,' I reply.

'That's if you don't do anything.'

Long arms reach in and drag Ilya from the taxi.

'Perhaps they'll just beat the crap out of *him*,' says the Doctor, slightly cheered.

Taran looks burdened with worry. He knows that Ilya is his friend and feels responsible for him. Ilya is now shouting that he's an American and can't be touched. Though he lives in New York, he remains an Uzbek Jew and his perfect Russian is unlikely to convince his abductors of his corn-bred claims. We turn to see him forced into the police car, two on either side of him, two in front. They pause by our taxi and indicate that we should follow.

'We could leave him,' says Doctor Tim, 'it's what he deserves.'

'Let's follow,' says Taran and uses one of his ten words of Russian to signal our intentions to the cab driver.

Meanwhile, the Doctor has used his cell phone to call a friend, relaying our movements turn by turn.

We stop in a dark side-street. Three of the police approach us and try to extract us from the taxi. The windows are rolled up.

Their tactics change. They start drawing numbers on their hands, then pressing their palms against the window: the amount of money they would like for Ilya's release.

We have no idea what's happening to Ilya inside the police car, but by the time we pull up to a police station, it is easy to see that he has been overcome by something, probably his own emotions, and is now weeping. He tries to come towards us. 'Pay them nothing. I will kill them all, kill them all, pay them nothing. They are dogs.'

Meanwhile, there is worse trouble than ours in the police station. About twenty cops are milling about outside in the warm evening, but their interest in us is dwindling. A young Azeri is trying to escort his girlfriend from the police station, apparently without permission from the police themselves. Voices are raised, about twenty of them. The young man takes a swing at the nearest cop and is suddenly covered in a swarm of blue shirts. This scrum moves back inside the station, leaving only a couple of policemen who have come to negotiate with us.

'I think they want a hundred and fifty,' says Doctor Tim.

We have only fifty dollars between us and that is smoothly palmed by the largest of the two policemen. He then tries for some local currency, but we plead ignorance. Ilya is released and comes towards us. After all the screaming, threats and antagonism, I'm astonished to see Ilya hug the most aggressive of the police officers. They pound each other on the back, Ilya wiping tears from his eyes as if they were reunited brothers.

In the taxi we ask, 'What did you tell them? What got them so angry?'

'I tell them', says Ilya, 'their country has lost much land in war, I tell them they should be ashamed. They should fight for country, not suck money on street like whore.'

Taran shakes his head in disbelief at the performance of his 'facilitator'. Troubles he had hoped to suppress throughout the journey are as obvious as fireworks at midnight.

If there's one theme to the next months, it is conflict: between ourselves, between those who surround us. With the problems of Dagestan and Chechnya boiling in the north, the threat is incessant. But every country in this region had been at war, even in the last dozen years.

As Ilya had pointed out to the policemen, Armenia had seized 20 per cent of Azerbaijan's land in Karabagh. Georgia had battled secession in Ossetia and Abkhazia, not to mention her fight for freedom against Russian forces. Most know of Russia's war against Chechnya that began in 1994, but blood has also been spilled in the neighbouring regions of Ingushetia and Dagestan. In short, the Caucasus region has been the most constant of the world's trouble spots. It is as if violence and bloodshed push up from the earth. There is no point pretending that the last decade's aggression stems from the time of Shamil. It goes back much further than that.

CHAPTER 3

# Back in Time

*We meet with Ramiz Norbalayev, who, fifteen years and a hundred pounds ago, used to be a middleweight boxer for Azerbaijan. He has a thick, black moustache, an eighty-a-day cigarette addiction and twenty words of English. He has also agreed to be our driver for the foreseeable future. We are moving at high speed towards Gobustan, home to Neolithic man some fourteen thousand years ago. Thick, black hair sprouts from Ramiz's collar like an Elizabethan ruff. Cigarette smoke trailing from his nostrils, he nods at us every now and then. His eyes are kind and shimmer, watering from his exhalations.*

We have been told to call our driver 'Mr Ramiz'. Among other things, he is a veteran of Azerbaijan's conflict against Armenia. He and Ilya are sitting up front swapping stories about their days in the Soviet army. Mr Ramiz seems to be a man of some importance. Every time that a policeman tries to flag us down for the usual non-existent offences, Mr Ramiz gives them a dismissive wave and then says in Russian, 'Sabaka droog chiloveka,' which roughly translates as 'A dog is a man's best friend.'

Ilya directs Mr Ramiz in a small detour to find a 'snake farm' marked on the map, which to his embarrassment turns out to be a secret military installation. Two hours later, with the morning's footage erased by a suspicious colonel, we are back on the road to Gobustan. 'I'm sorry, my friends,' Ilya shrugs.

Gobustan is to be found in a landscape of mud volcanoes, coughing cold fluids upwards. They are rarely dangerous, the last fatality coming after the Second World War when a huge gas build-up ruptured the earth, sending rocks, six shepherds and five hundred sheep into the sky. Fourteen thousand years ago, the Caspian was connected to the Black Sea. The environment around the western shores of the Caspian was very different: wooded, thick with game and home to one of the earliest known colonies of Neolithic man. The caves of Gobustan are formed in the sides of a rocky plateau, at the base of a sheer drop. Their walls are covered with carved depictions of cattle, deer, whales, insects, shamen and, most mysteriously, what appear to be Viking long-ships.

The explorer Thor Heyerdahl has recently visited Gobustan. He rubbed toothpaste into the grooves of the cave paintings to make them easier to distinguish. Heyerdahl theorizes that the original Caucasians, blond-haired and blue-eyed, were driven from their Caspian hunting grounds by the Arab armies of the eighth century. Sailing from the Caspian, they moved through the Black Sea, out through the Dardanelles into the open sea and north. The timing of this exodus coincides with Norse tales of the visitors from the south, who came bearing knowledge of ships and ocean currents. In short, Heyerdahl believes that the Vikings are descended from the cave dwellers of Gobustan.

The strange paintings may or may not be longships, but there is no doubting the images of deer and cattle. The Gobustan hunting technique was simple: the men would drive game on to the highest point, calling, shouting, using bursts of speed to push the animals forward. Tightening the circle, the hunters would charge their prey: some of the animals would double back, breaking through the lines of men, while others would simply leap from the plateau, falling 150 feet down to the rocks near the openings of the caves. It was a simple manoeuvre, imitated in abattoirs across Europe until the twentieth century, known as the knacker's drop. The animal would break its legs, or perhaps its neck. All that remained was for the throat to be cut. While in Europe this task would be left to bloodied men in aprons, in Gobustan the paintings suggest that it was the women and children who delivered the final blow.

They would walk among the fallen animals, sharpened stone in hand, braining or slitting throats. It was a brutal and effective management, leaving the carcasses a short drag from the caves. There they could be skinned and gutted in safety, by the light of fire.

# CHAPTER 4

# Reverberation

*There is perhaps one incident early in Shamil's war against the*

*Russians that brings to mind the lessons of Gobustan. If it is*

*not a repetition of technique, then it is certainly an echo. The*

*second siege of Akhulgo is considered by historians to be the*

*turning point of the war.*

Akhulgo, two hundred miles north of Gobustan, was divided into two parts, built upon a pair of uneven rocky heads, each crowned with an *aoul*, the name given to the fortified mountain villages of the Caucasus. Though the two settlements were close enough to shoot an arrow from one *aoul* to another, they were separated by both a steep drop and a fast-running river. In 1839 Shamil had retreated to Akhulgo and mustered his forces: the last time he was to do so, for it was exactly what the Russian command sought – an opportunity to rout the mountaineers with a single blow.

After the third week of the siege, General Grabbe, the Tsar's latest choice to subdue the Caucasus, was informed that Shamil had decided to flee his citadel. It did not surprise him. Though it was a cool June day of blue skies and fresh wind, the stench of the

Muslim dead from the continual bombardment drifted all the way down to the Russian encampment in the valley below. Shamil's troops would not dispose of their brothers' bodies indiscriminately. Each corpse awaited a ceremonial burial.

Despite the appalling conditions within Akhulgo, Grabbe's information was incorrect. He opted to send three columns to flush the opposition from within walls already blasted by Russian artillery. The first column moved along a narrow ridge beneath the higher *aoul* and was forced into single file, the scaling ladders held above the soldiers' heads. They were aiming for a flat, open platform, just beneath the elevated section of Akhulgo. Grabbe had decided it would make the perfect starting point for their assault. The column was fired on first from a position beneath the lower of the *aouls*, hurrying them towards the platform, and then more fiercely from the higher fortification so that they did not know which way to turn.

There were six hundred Russians driven on to this open wedge beneath the elevated *aoul*. On either side was a fall of several hundred feet, ahead a sheer rock face leading up to Akhulgo, behind them the narrow ledge which they now knew lay open to fire from the lower *aoul*. The mountaineers did not wait for the Russians to realize the helplessness of their position, but continued to fire. Russian officers were dressed differently to their troops. Their coats were often lined with brocade, making them easier to identify during a march, or even across a chasm. The Muslim sharpshooters picked off the officers first, then began on their charges, leaving the platform slippery with blood. The Russians were herded close to one another, screaming for order, but no orders came. There were no officers left alive.

The second column moved up towards the lower *aoul* of Akhulgo. They could hear that the firing had ceased to the east but were hidden from sight of the first column by the rise of the land.

Many on the exposed platform were dead, but several hundred survived, though they had little to protect themselves save the bodies of their comrades. The enemy had ceased firing, not out of any sympathy for the Russians' predicament, but because they thought it a waste of ammunition. A turn in weather might account for many by morning.

The second column must have had no warning as they walked along the thin ridge beneath the lower *aoul*. Boulders came rushing down upon them. Great rocks lifted men off the path, pulverizing them or jettisoning small groups down the ravine. Within a matter of minutes, the narrow ledge was clogged with bodies and rocks, blocking the path altogether. The rest of the troops retreated.

The final column made its way to the foot of the elevated *aoul*, attacking from a northern position that prevented them from seeing the fate of their fellow soldiers. They were now so close that the smell of the Muslim dead must have convinced them that the enemy was exhausted. They could not know that most of the firing they had heard was directed at their own troops. As they passed along the final twist of the ledge before the village entrance, they were attacked. Women and children leapt on them from higher ground. The children clasped their native *kinjals*, a long, curved dagger carried by all their fathers. They kept low to the ground, thrusting upwards into the bellies of their foe. The women were dressed in the clothes of their husbands or fathers, in an attempt to deceive the Russians.

The soldiers who survived this attack were struck by both the ferocity of the attack and the commitment to death. Women would snatch at a soldier as they fell over the precipice, happy to perish if they might swap life for life. The Russians also remembered that the bodies of dead children were thrown against them. They retreated, now certain that Shamil had no plans to flee from Akhulgo.

Hunting, warfare and bloodshed may have been dominated by men, but violence was not their exclusive domain. In desperate times, the thousands of years that separated Gobustan and Akhulgo evaporated. In both eras the entire family took any advantages that the land might have to offer them and life, if anything, was worth less than that land. Children were used as rocks; it may be horrifying but it also suggests that the boundaries that divide mountains from mountaineers were at their most fragile in the Caucasus.

Long before the Islamic laws of the Sharia were heard through the Caucasus, it was a largely animist region, paying strict obedience to the Adats. The Adats were an evolving form of ancestral custom that doubled as law, centred on the abilities of clans and families to deal with their own. They were revered even before the written word. Festivals were, as in most animist religions, based on the seasons of the natural world: moon, harvests, snows. Grapes and milk were fermented, then drunk. Even after Islam took its first steps in the foothills of the Caucasus, it was not until the time of Shamil that a disdain for alcohol was cultivated.

The custom of the Adats coexisted with Islamic teachings in the days of Shamil and they continue to live side by side today. These were laws that had evolved over time, passed in the oral tradition from one generation to another. They may have been so ancient that no man knew their roots, but they were not doubted. They contained a dignity and rough order that merged independence with respect, even for the dead. Tremendous importance is placed upon a man being buried in his village, next to all his ancestors. It was in Chechnya in the 1990s as it was in Akhulgo in 1839. In both cases neutrals observed men being wounded and even dying while fighting for the reclamation of a dead soldier.

Many of the mountaineers, and especially the Chechens, have long been divided into *teips* or extended families. Unlike the neighbouring countries, there is no elite in the Chechen mountains, no contained body that might be killed, corrupted or otherwise stained to shake a nation. The West has nothing as comparatively resilient and as egalitarian as the *teip*. It is the right of every man to claim equality with his neighbour, though within a lifetime valour might bring fame and respect. According to John Baddeley, traveller in and historian of the Caucasus, 'No Chechen ever attained to supreme authority in his own country, or even his own district.'[2]

To the traveller, from Dumas to Tolstoy, it is the code of vendetta that has stood out among the customs of the Adat. Revenge is a right and an honour. It was not so much eye for eye and tooth for tooth as eyes for eye and teeth for tooth. At first, it seems savage and outdated, but as Alexander Solzhenitsyn says:

> perhaps not so senseless after all. It does not sap the moun-
> tain peoples, but strengthens them. Not so very many fall
> victim to the law of vendetta – but what power the fear
> of it has all around. With this law in mind, no highlander
> will casually insult another, as we insult each other in drink,
> from lack of self-control or just for the hell of it . . . Strike
> your neighbors, that strangers may fear you. The ancestors
> of the highlanders in remote antiquity could have found no
> stronger hoop to gird their people.[3]

The problem with the vendetta is that once started, it is hard to stop. There are many examples within Caucasian history of blood feuds going back four and five generations. Though Shamil drew some of his power from the Adats and recognized how they had strengthened the people of the mountains, he preached openly against the blood feud, often ridiculing it. He liked to tell the story, apocryphal as it may be, of two neighbours in the village of Kadar.

One stole a hen from the other. The second responded by thieving a sheep. The first then stole two sheep, infuriating his neighbour, who graduated to absconding with a cow. The first now passed all sense of propriety and stole his neighbour's horse. Nothing equals the importance of a man's horse, so the exasperated man was forced to kill his neighbour and then promptly disappeared. The kin of the victim responded by murdering his closest relation and back and forth they went, generation to generation. According to Shamil, several hundred had now died over a hen. If Solzhenitsyn makes a good case of mutual disarmament over the threat of vendetta then Shamil parodies its potential damage.

The blood feud did, of course, lead to suspicion and unease between different *teips*. After committing a crime, one of the few ways to avoid a blood feud was to establish yourself as an *abrek*, as integral a part of the Adats as the vendetta itself. There is no perfect translation for *abrek*, though in Russian it is happily interpreted as 'bandit'. Traditionally, these outcasts gathered high in the hills, living a rough, unsheltered life in harsh conditions. They were feared, but also respected among their own people. It was part of the code of the *abrek* that once the oath was taken, it would last a lifetime. It also insured that the *abrek* would never work the fields again. How, then, did they eat? They stole, in keeping with the laws of the Adats. Baddeley, who travelled in the 1890s through the Caucasus, commented, 'Cattle lifting, highway robbery and murder were, in this strange code, counted deeds of honour; . . . these, together with fighting against any foe, but especially the hated Russian, were the only pursuits deemed worthy of a grown man.'[4]

What is extraordinary is that Baddeley was not just referring to the *abreks* themselves, but to all men who lived in the mountain villages. The ideals and objectives of the competing lands of Russia and the Caucasus could not have been more different. Russia, whether under the Tsar or Soviet rule, was led from above, land hungry, thirsting for conquests that might in turn father conquests. The irony was that they chose to conquer a people who had long believed that from the moment of birth the only traits to be valued in a man were bravery and skill in combat. It was a conflict of cultures at the most basic of levels.

# CHAPTER 5

# Living History

*About two hundred miles from Baku, we are, once again, reasonably lost. Mr Ramiz and Ilya have developed a strange relationship of shared cigarettes and head slapping and have begun to resemble a post-Soviet Laurel and Hardy routine. We no longer know where we are going. The map we are using was produced by the Soviets in the mid-Brezhnev era and has not taken into account the disintegration of mountain roads. We bump past broken-down buses, winding our way through densely wooded hills. It's hard to know if that is mist rolling down the mountains, or just cigarette smoke from the front seat.*

John and I are wedged in the back seat, Taran luxuriates in front. 'I need to film,' he explains, which would be understandable except for the fact that he always seems to be sleeping. There is, already, a shipboard feeling of claustrophobia. Groups have formed, which the captain must always rise above. It's all worryingly petty, but as a form of survival, effective.

The Caucasus, among many of its other claims, is supposedly

home to the oldest humans in the world. Every village we stop in, we roll up to a gathering of men and ask them if they happen to have an aged grandparent close by.

'My father is very old,' says one man.

'How old?'

'Eighty-two,' he replies.

This happens again and again, the ages rising to the late nineties, then dipping back into the eighties. Finally, standing amid a group of mulling middle-aged men, a short young man peers upwards at us. 'My great-grandfather is very, very old.'

'How old?'

'One hundred and twenty-eight.'

John raises first one eyebrow, then the other, but it is, after all, what we wanted to hear.

You can count on hospitality in the Caucasus. Strangers are welcomed as family, a fact that is both warming and disconcerting. Passing over a muddied stoop we peeled our boots from our feet and entered the front room. The family gathered about us. There were five generations present. Dozens of flies circled a bowl of sugar that stood alone on a table in the centre of the room. Chairs were brought from about the house and we stayed seated, smiling uncomfortably and sipping at cups of tea. It seems to be the custom of the region not to mix the sugar and the tea, but to swallow lumps of sweetness after every sip or so. While the people of the Caucasus may live to great ages, evidently their teeth do not. Everywhere, we are greeted by gap-toothed grins.

The patriarch walked in. Though his face was deeply lined, his hands atremble and his progress slow, he walked unaided. He looked very much like the ringed trunk of an ancient tree. Shaking our hands with a firm grip, he then motioned for us to sit and took his place at the head of the table. He did not speak Russian, only the local Azeri dialect, and our interview became a game of cross-cultural Chinese whispers.

'How old are you?'

'One hundred twenty-eight.'

'We don't mean to be rude, but can you prove your age?'

'Yes, you have my word.'

'That is very fine. Is there any documentation? For the camera.'

There is. A Stalin-era identity card issued to every man in the Soviet Union. It is dated 1934, at which time our host was identified as a man of sixty-two years of age.

Ilya leans over. 'Very old man. But Stalin times, maybe somebody ask him how old you are and he say "I don't know," they say, "You look very old, like sixty-two," but maybe he not so old, maybe he just fifty years back then. Maybe he young now. Just one hundred and sixteen.'

'Ask him what was the strangest encounter of his life.'

'It is an easy answer,' he says.

For some reason I think he is going to talk of Shamil.

'I have met the Forest Man.'

John whispers in my ear, 'It's a Caucasus myth, just like the yeti.'

'Would you tell us the story?'

'I was coming through my fields when I saw him. He was very hairy.'

We wait for more, but that's it.

Taran turns to Ilya. 'Ask him to what he attributes his extraordinary longevity.' Taran has the habit, when asking Ilya to translate, of choosing a series of words designed to show the limitations of his own translator.

'My English no understands,' says Ilya.

John laughs at Taran. 'Ilya, ask him how come he's lived so long.'

'It is an easy answer,' says the ancient. 'I live in the mountains. I do not drink. I do not smoke. I have many, many children, but also four wives. They age, I do not.'

In the 1960s the Soviets sent a group of scientists to this region to conduct a series of blood tests in an attempt to unravel the secret to longevity. There were no answers; old age was generally attributed to clean air, water and a stress-free lifestyle. Old age did, however, seem to be genetic. Families gave rise to centenarian after centenarian as if each generation had a responsibility to endure. Perhaps equally important is the fact that age, not just great age, made a person more important within each family structure. There was and is no concept of retirement in these mountains. Elders not only work but are also seen as the custodians of culture, expected to attend all the rites of life as well as transferring their knowledge to the succeeding generations. According to the villagers, the worst curse that one can wish upon another family is 'May your house be empty of elders when you wish for guidance'.

If Bandiev Kishi was indeed 128 years old, then he would have been born in the year that Shamil died: a single leap through five generations of political movements; a man who had seen both the rise and fall of the Soviets.

# CHAPTER 6

# Born in the Land of Splintered Stars

*If the Caucasus was not fully conquered when Kishi was a child,*

*it was only because of Shamil. And while Kishi's earliest memory*

*may have been of mountains diverse in language and heritage,*

*the same was true of Shamil's early years. Only in the inter-*

*ceding years, between the birth of Shamil in 1797 and the birth*

*of our ancient friend, could the tribes of the Caucasus ever have*

*been said to work together. By the 1870s, after the defeat of*

*Shamil, the laws of the mountains rose up out of the ashes of*

*the holy war, and because of the re-emergence of the Adats, the*

*two men might have shared many experiences in childhood.*

In the mountains, the Adats themselves were mostly oral histories. Each tribe had its own set of regulations; rather like state laws that worked within federal law, they met and crossed, differed but had so much in common that compromises were generally reached. One of the traditions that many *teips* and tribes shared was the *ashlik*, a wandering storyteller. This Caucasian troubadour was always a welcomed guest in the villages of the mountains. Some of these settlements were so remote that they lay on the road to nowhere but the skies above. Accidental and incidental visitors were unheard of. The arrival of the *ashlik* was a cause for celebration. Perhaps the winter snows had only just melted, perhaps they were about to fall and it had been over a year since a visitor had passed through the village. Shamil was born in Avaria, an area now bisected by the border of Azerbaijan and Dagestan. Not the most remote of locations, but still, a journey of many days into the mountains. As a child, Shamil would have been among the outer ring of listeners. The elders would have poured the *ashlik* wine; if the winter's tobacco had not been exhausted, then smoke would have risen from the party, like clouds hanging over mountaintops. When all were gathered, the *ashlik* would begin.

Many years ago, when the earth was young, it was so flat that as the sea grew violent it would always swamp the lands, often drowning animals and men. The Creator wanted there to be rivers, but there could be no rivers without hills. He decided to give every land its share of mountains, choosing to divide them equally among nations. He put them all in a sack, but the Devil knew that they were too fine a gift to be given to men, so as the Creator flew between the Black and the Caspian seas, he slit the sack and the mountains crashed down, one upon the other, rising towards the heavens. The Creator was angry. He turned to the Devil and forbade him from ever setting foot on these peaks. For the men who would live there, declared the Creator, would have hard enough lives as it was.

The moral of the story was simple: the hills were reserved for princes, bandits and the noble people. Living on the plain was, in every sense, a descent. Down there the life was easy, but there were reasons to fear those who lived above. The mountaineers were purer, stronger and closer to the gods, subject to jealousy, respect and dread from below.

One story was not enough, no matter how long the *ashlik* would spin his tale. Though Noah may have saved the animals of the earth, the Caucasian version of the myth has a significant addition. No one knew just how high the waters would rise. When they reached so high that great portions of the earth were inundated, two people from each nation were hidden among the peaks of the Caucasus. It was said that the people were so different from one another that they shared neither looks nor language. It is from these tribes that all the mountain races are descended, though they were forbidden by God to breed in heavy numbers. They were to remain apart from the rest of humanity. The valleys had been chosen to host the new, diluted races of man. The mountains, and the people that lived there, were to stand as a monument to God's mercy and his vengeance. This showed not only that the highlanders thought of themselves as older and better than those from the plains, but also that there might exist a brotherhood among the mountaineers.

Perhaps it was this story that sparked Shamil's imagination, showing that there stood a chance of accord and a mutual pact of resistance between such diverse groups of people. Then again, Shamil may have reacted against these stories, even as a young man. Both he and his best friend, Ghazi Mullah, began studying the Koran as children. We know that from a young age Shamil harboured great disdain for the customs of the mountains that contradicted the Sharia, or laws of the Koran. That alcohol was used widely could not surprise him, but the fact that his father was a drunk was both humiliating and sinful. The boy challenged his father over his drinking, said that he would kill himself should he ever find his father drunk again. It is hard to know what the father saw within his son's eyes that made him believe the boy, but it was the last drink that he ever took.

Shamil was not as strong as the other children. He began life as a sickly, weak boy who answered to the name Ali. In Ghimri, the village of his birth, it was the custom that an ailing child might have his name changed. Ali became Shamil and subsequently recovered, though his inability to participate in the games of his fellow youths had resulted in a greater understanding of Arabic and book learning. Now that he was capable of competing with his peers he did not hesitate. It was said that at the age of twenty he out-jumped all the young men of the village in reaching the mark of twenty-seven feet.

Wrestling and dance, as in most countries, were learned in play. But at an age when most of the Western educators were teaching the Greek alphabet, the Caucasian child was learning the use of sword, bow and gun. It was not without precedent, certainly the Spartan education was just as bellicose. As with the Spartans, thieving was also considered an art, concentrating on the ability to remain calm, to move silently, to retain daring. 'The principal object', said the historian J. Milton Mackie of the Caucasian education, 'was to form an accomplished warrior.'[5]

However, unlike the Spartans, the Chechens and tribes of Dagestan thought it beneath a man to fight as a foot soldier. The impressive Veliamenov, architect of much of Russia's early movement in the Caucasus, noted the difference between his famed Cossacks, Russia's frontier cavalry, and his new adversaries.

The mounted natives are very superior in many ways both to our regular cavalry and the Cossacks. They are all but born on horseback, and, being used to riding from their earliest years, become extremely expert in this art, and are accustomed to covering great distances without fatigue.[6]

He went on to say that their horses were capable of travelling over a hundred miles between dawn and dusk. This would have made your average Victorian scoff and raise an eyebrow. How could one horse, birthed a thousand miles from Dover, travel twice as far as his thoroughbred?

Horses were allowed to roam wild in the forests for part of the year, contending with bear and wolf and attaining natural resistance to the harshest elements the Caucasus Mountains could conjure. Subduing the horses was in itself an act of horsemanship, an opportunity for precocious children to prove themselves to their elders. The horses were trained for raiding, and though many preferred to condition their own, the duty would often fall to young men, such as Shamil. For two months before the first of the season's raids was scheduled, the horse was fattened, then the amount of food was gradually diminished. Every day the horse was ridden, though never hard, then left up to its middle in cold water for several hours. Initially, the stallion was walked, then slowly progressed to a trot until the layer of fat was seen to melt, leaving the horse muscular and able to gallop long distances at a time. Never was the horse laden with equipment: the only food a raider might take was a couple of handfuls of millet.

The connection felt between mountaineer and horse was as ancient as their myths. George Sava, a Georgian author, records a Caucasian legend that asks, 'Who were my ancestors? He who pulled milk out of a wild mare's udder with his lips and grew drunk as a little foal.'[7]

In the fifth century BC, Herodotus had been sent to the Black Sea region, perhaps by Pericles. He was the first Greek who looked beyond the typical notion of Greeks and non-Greeks. Contemporaries, such as Euripides, equated foreignness with barbarity. The Scythians were considered the most savage of all, vicious nomads directly opposed to the Greek notion of permanent city-states. Herodotus wrote, 'I do not admire everything about the

Scythians, but in this supreme concern they have invented a system which means that nobody who attacks them can escape and can catch them if they do not wish to be found.' This was much later echoed by Veliamenov's sentiments regarding the mountaineers. The tactics were identical: lure the enemy onwards, driving your horses deep into the harsh lands that nurtured you and drawing the enemy far enough from their cities to blur the lines of hunters and hunted. At a Scythian burial ground in Ulskii, preserved for archaeologists by permafrost, the carcasses of 360 horses were found forming a ring about the royal dead. Brightly coloured saddle cloths and horse-masks filled the tombs. In history and myth, the region connected man and horse both in birth and in death.

The second part of Shamil's education seems in direct contrast to such bucolic physicality. With Ghazi Mullah, he left the village of Ghimri for Yaragul to study the Koran under the greatest teachers in all of Dagestan. In Yaragul, the lessons learned were not those of the Adats. Together, Shamil and Ghazi Mullah studied Arabic, read from the Koran and began to preach as one against the evils of drink. They were seen to beat one another with rods in public for confessing that they had in their lives tasted wine, before understanding the gravity of their sins.

At the same time, an event in Chechnya, less than a hundred miles from Ghimri, would also help to shape the course of Shamil's life. Yermolov was possibly the most famous of nineteenth-century Russian generals: he may not have been solely responsible for the Russian victories over France in 1812, but somehow he had emerged as the figurehead of conquest. In the eyes of the Russian public, he could do no wrong. The Tsar sent him to the Caucasus, and Pushkin heralded his arrival: 'Submit and bow your snowy head, O Caucasus, Yermolov marches.'

One of his first acts in the mountains was to build a fort that he would call Grozny, Russian for 'formidable'. It marked the boundary between Russia's frontier, called the Cossack Line, and those who, for a while at least, were known as the 'peaceable Chechens'. The Chechens raided in this area as a way of life, and it was this constant harassing of the Cossack Line that first prompted Yermolov to build his fort.

The Russians and the Chechens had very different concepts of land. In Chechnya, there was no ownership of land and therefore the idea of conquering and possessing territory was alien to them. However, the erection of the fort at Grozny was interpreted as an aggressive act, if not of ownership, then of intent and permanence. Every night, those involved in the construction of the fort would have to brave constant sniping. Yermolov decided to punish a raiding party. A field gun was deliberately abandoned by the Russians at a predetermined spot. All remaining guns were trained on it. That night, 10 June 1818, a large raiding party descended to seize the prize. They were met by a barrage of shot. Not knowing from which direction they were being fired on, they stood for a moment, then the survivors bent over to pick up their dead and wounded. In this time, the Russians had been able to reload and delivered a second storm of grape shot. Yermolov wrote to the Tsar, 'Two hundred dead and as many wounded . . . served as a good lesson, and for a long time took away the appetite for night attacks.' It was Yermolov, speaking half a century before the American General Sheridan, who coined the transmutable term, 'the only good Chechen is a dead Chechen'.

Life on the Cossack Line was tense, often dull, occasionally bloody, but raids in the early days rarely resulted in even a single death. Yermolov's brutal example was definitive. It ensured that for the next fifty years the Russians would encounter nothing but hatred and suspicion. How long does hate last? One hundred and seventy-six years later, in 1994, Grozny's declaration of independence was signalled by the demolition of Yermolov's statue. Nobody had forgotten. It took three charges to reduce the old general, but he eventually fell.

Back in Ghimri, Ghazi Mullah and Shamil heard the reports of Russian progress in the foothills, of the slow encroachment of unbelievers. Yermolov's efforts coincided exactly with the young men's education, causing what was simply a form of religious zeal to grow alongside a heated patriotism. Religion was one of the few reasons for men to leave their villages, to exchange ideas with neighbours. Perhaps it was natural, then, that resistance should grow around those who stood behind the Koran and called for change. In the lowlands, the Adats had done nothing to help repel the Russians. Why not follow the Sharia, adhere to the strict Islamic laws and be backed against the unbelievers by Allah himself?

Shamil remained unsettled. In Ghimri, he continued to study the Koran, in particular the Tarikat, or correct path, under Jamal Uddin. Ghazi Mullah was quick to call for Ghazavat, a holy war against the infidel. Shamil was not so sure, heavily influenced by Jamal Uddin, who was to become not only his teacher, but his father-in-law. The discussions over action became heated and Ghazi Mullah resolved to return to the elders of Yaragul. The question he asked, in retrospect, seems weighted towards his desired answer.

'God commands us to fight the infidel and the unbeliever, but Jamal Uddin refuses this sanction. Whose commands shall I obey?'

The answer was simple. 'Obey the commands of God rather than those of men.'

Ghazi Mullah had his wish. Wisely, he did not immediately declare the holy war that he had been agitating for. Under the guise of a simple religious reformer, Ghazi Mullah travelled the countryside for several years as the First Imam of Dagestan. Only when his support had grown and Russian intent on conquest had become clear to all did he contemplate the proclamation of a holy war. Shamil stood by his side, his first *naib*, or lieutenant. Their task was close to impossible. Not only were they to resist the most powerful army in Europe, but they were to do so in a region splintered by hundreds of years of tribal warfare, where languages could differ from one mountaintop to the next.

# CHAPTER 7

# Three Hundred Tongues

*Far above the town of Quba is the tiny village of Deuaie, cradled*

*between two soft peaks, little brothers of the mountains behind*

*them. Just south of the Dagestani border with Azerbaijan, we*

*have stopped off on the northern road to visit a friend of Taran's.*

*A year ago, Taran travelled up these hills on foot. Today we arrive*

*in a Jeep and are chased the final yards by a flock of small*

*children dressed in bright wool clothes and rubber boots.*

Mamet is at home and greets Taran as if he had been expecting him for weeks, though without a phone he could have had no warning of our arrival. Once again, it is the law of hospitality that prevails. Children are scattered in all directions through the village and up the hill, sent with messages to brothers and cousins that a sheep will be roasted for the guests.

We are escorted up the incline, John led up bareback on a small horse. He laughs away at the rest of us. We are now high enough above sea level for exercise to have become an unattractive proposition. Mamet has run ahead, hopping from rock to rock and through the long grasses like an ibex. I pause to wipe the sweat from my eyes and readjust John's cameras over my shoulders. Mamet's nephew notices my discomfort. The hills are dusted with wild flowers, specks coloured like setting suns and harvest moons. The young man plucks the purple flowers and holds them to my nose. They smell of concentrated jasmin but have a mentholated purity about them. One deep inhalation is equal to a third lung. He explains, in English, Russian and gesture, that they can be made into tea to cure heart palpitations and altitude sickness. I fill a pocket with purple flowers while he laughs and stoops to help me.

A half-mile from his brother's house, Mamet stops our party by the side of a stream. Trees stand over our heads, providing shelter from the sun. The locals flatten out a bed of wild flowers and drop a thick woollen blanket amid the grass. Within ten minutes, relatives emerge from upstream and downstream. A babushka negotiates the stepping stones across the water, holding a spade filled with burning embers before her. The fire is started, but, very gently, rain begins to fall, first like a mist, then in discernible drops. The nephew breaks off a series of dock leaves from the edge of the stream and, attaching them to a wooden pole, creates a protective cover over the flames. Lamb, vodka, cucumbers, tomatoes, bread and cheese appear from all directions. One of the children rummages in the grass behind us and returns with spring onions he has just pulled from the earth. Ilya bites into a bulb with an audible crunch and laughs at its freshness. 'Not New York. This Kavkaz,' he says, using the Russian word for these mountains.

Toasts accompany each shot of vodka and though the rain continues to fall it disturbs no one. The road, it is agreed, will now be unpassable. Any rockslide could sweep a vehicle off the sides of the mountain. In places, it is over a thousand feet to the river bed. With the decision to spend the night in Denare made, we continue to drink until everyone is so drunk that the decision is reversed. It is, everyone agrees, not raining that hard.

Mr Ramiz growls his way into the driver's seat and Mamet sits beside him, deciding to accompany us ever upwards. The distinct smell of fatted lamb is on everybody's breath. In the crushed back seat a row of cigarettes is lit to dispel the aroma. A mile upstream, where the road seems to climb upwards while the river slopes down, we are already at least five hundred feet above the water. Beneath us, washed over by white water, is the carcass of another Jeep. Instead of causing any worry, we all find rocks and try to bounce them off the body of the vehicle far below.

John has taken the seat furthest away from the drop. He has a small problem with vertigo. His fingers keep finding their way to his new goatee, tugging anxiously at the growth. 'Stupid, no?' mutters John. 'Photographer on a mountain expedition is afraid of heights.'

Now we are among the mountains. The path is no wider than the Jeep but the vodka seems to be having a beneficial effect on Mr Ramiz, who is attacking the track in high gears. John, despite occasional laughter, has looked better. Three mountains lock ahead of us. Mamet makes us stop the car and Taran begins to film. 'This', says Mamet, 'is the gateway to the true Caucasus.' Embarrassed clouds can only make it halfway up these peaks. Their tops lie above the rain. Both the mountains and the ice that cloaks them are older than man.

We are heading for Hinaliq, a village not twenty miles away that Mamet has only visited once in his life. Though he lives in the closest village, he does not speak their language. As we wind slowly upwards, we rise over a crest that had blocked our vision to the east. Having just made our way across ravines and yawning chasms, it is strange to find ourselves back on level ground with the stream, which now broadens into a churning river. Beyond it is yet another group of mountains.

Another hour onwards, the mountains relent, the river having carved a flood plain along a high valley. Against the setting sun, the men and women of Hinaliq are working the fields. They stand to watch us pass, their scythes planted upright in the soil, silhouetted against the sun. Finally, we see the village ahead. Like Shamil's *aouls* it is built into the side of a mountain, the back of each house formed from the mountain itself. With the end of the day, Hinaliq looks both beautiful and ominous.

We pause in the centre of the village before a line of unmoving elders. It is a strange combination: the thin air, the stone streets and silent faces, the village balanced on top of the world, clouds below. For a moment everything is still. Ilya walks in a small circle smiling. It's a Caucasian fairy tale. Suddenly, we are engulfed by children who burst around the corner of a stone house, shouting and squirting water at us. None of the elders rises. They still look on, neither repelling nor welcoming us. Taran spots a man who befriended him the year before, named Avass. He is short, with a moustache that stands off his face like a stiff brush. One by one, we are introduced to the elders, who sit like a line of gargoyles on their bench, each one capped with a large white sheepskin hat, called a *papakh*.

Avass also speaks Russian. 'The elders', he asks, 'wish to know if you are selling anything?'

We shake our heads and are led by our host down a narrow lane towards his house. Everything is built of stone from the mountains: the cobbled street, each house.

'How old is your house?' we ask Avass when we stand before his home.

'I don't know,' he says. 'My grandfather's grandfather lived here and he did not know either. It is always in my family.'

The view is extraordinary. We are ringed by mountains in every direction. The steep pastures of the village lie to the west, small flocks of sheep and goat being driven back to Hinaliq in the dying light.

Avass's home is dark, covered in carpets, the ceilings low to keep warmth contained. During a dinner of yogurt and herb soup he tells how six years ago he lay paralysed, the left side of his body frozen. He did not know how it had happened, but confessed that he used to drink great quantities of vodka. He had woken one morning and could not move, could not leave the village to tend his flock, could not earn money to keep his family. For a year he lay there. One night he dreamed that Imam Shamil appeared before him, holding a bowl of water in his hands. Avass drank from the bowl. After his first sip, the water was transformed into brightly coloured flowers. When he awoke, he had recovered completely. Out of respect for Shamil, he has not touched alcohol since. Despite this claim, he finds a bottle in his house and encourages us in our toasts. Ilya surprises us all in the poetry of his toast. When he sits, he says, 'Don't worry, this mountains. Drink, drink, no can get drunk in mountains. Always feel good in morning.'

All Avass's guests sleep in a row, the five of us covered in bright woollen blankets, lying against one another, a cacophony of snores. Taran has been smiling to himself for hours. It seems that the further we get above sea level the happier he becomes. Perhaps it is also because he now has Ilya far enough from the city to lessen the odds of conflict. We're still dressed in dumb smiles, a natural drunkenness from being in a place that surpasses your imagination, pushing you back 150 years into the past.

In the middle of the night I rise to attempt to find the bathroom. It is outside the house, down a black alley, over the stray chickens. At the edge of the cliff turn right. It is, without a doubt, the most dangerous outhouse in the world, balanced in loose stone on the edge of a five-hundred-foot drop. The hole that has been carved in its centre is just big enough for a man to slip through. It would be the most ignominious of ends.

In the morning Avass tells us that the last visitors from the West to the village of Hinaliq came just after the fall of the Iron Curtain. They were a pair of linguists who stayed a year and left unable to interpret what they had heard. There are such diverse explanations for the languages of the Caucasus that no single one makes sense; the answer is most probably an assortment of choices. One of the Russian names for the Caucasus is 'the mountain of languages'. Pliny quoted Timosthenes noting that the ancient Greeks counted three hundred separate languages of the Caucasus. He continued that the Romans, in his day, travelled with a mere 130 interpreters. In neighbouring villages professors have found Turkic, Indo-European and Caucasian tongues. Quite how this happened no one knows. According to myth, God stumbled while dividing nationalities and spilled far too many in the mountains. History is about as helpful, different schools adhering to warring theories. Some have it that Alexander the Great used the Caucasus as the dumping ground to exile the murderers, bandits and least desirable men from his armies. The Persians also pushed into the mountains, often enough to give rise to the phrase 'When a shah is a fool, he attacks Dagestan.' The Turkish empire included swathes of the southern Caucasus, as did the Mongol, Armenian and Russian empires. Germans colonized a small portion of central Georgia. Christianity took root in Ossetian lands, bringing with it scraps of Latin. The Kharvasurs wore chain mail with a red cross painted in the centre right until the beginning of the twentieth century. It was a part of their heritage, purportedly as descendants of lost crusaders.

While the Caucasus had been passed through by some of the

greatest armies the world had ever seen, it was always host to a series of overlapping conquerors. Muscovy princes were ousted by the Arabs, who were swept aside by Tamerlane until finally, in the nineteenth century there remained only three recognizable powers: Persia, Turkey and Russia. But the mountains themselves had belonged to no empire: they may have been coloured in on generals' charts, but throughout these generations, myriad cultures survived. If all successful revolutions have to begin culturally, then the mountains and those who lived in them contained in the 1820s an undefeated people, their independence and ethics very much intact.

This is the land that Russia chose to invade and that Ghazi Mullah and Shamil sought to unite. The only tongue that connected village to village was Arabic, the language of the Koran. Few knew the scriptures as well as Ghazi Mullah, who had committed to memory over four hundred of the *Ahadis*, or religious epigrams, giving him ample ammunition in debates. His reputation as a holy man spread through the mountains, and still keeping his desires for war buried, he accepted invitations from various khanates and communities, those loyal to the Tsar and those with no declared allegiance. To those who listened closely, his words could lead only to war, but with Russia distracted by her campaigns in both Turkey and Persia, Ghazi Mullah was considered nothing more than a potential inconvenience. He travelled until 1829, when in Ghimri, the village of his birth, with Shamil beside him, he announced the beginning of the holy war, calling to all those who had heard him speak to join as one against the infidels.

# CHAPTER 8

# The First Imam

*Shamil and Ghazi Mullah's first move, symbolic of the discord of the mountains, was against a former teacher. Raiding his* aoul, *they burned his books, those written and those collected throughout a lifetime. From the area surrounding this town of Arakani, Ghazi Mullah took hostages, sending them back to Ghimri where they were incarcerated in underground pits. It is obvious that from the early days of the conflict, acts of terror were to play at least as great a part in co-opting the support of their countrymen as was the word of Allah. Urging a meeting of the religious leaders of Dagestan at Ghimri, Ghazi Mullah was unsurprisingly confirmed as the country's First Imam.*

The considerable forces that gathered around Ghazi Mullah and Shamil suffered their first defeat at the hands of the men of Khounzakh, a band of refugees who saw no appeal in the puritanical brand of Islam that the Murids, or holy warriors, marched under. Perhaps it would have been more difficult to gather a large army again had not the Russians launched their own offensive, seeking to exploit the split that sundered Dagestan.

The Russian army that had been established in the Caucasus region numbered, in the early days of what came to be called the Murid Wars, around 75,000 (increased from 50,000 by Yermolov who well understood the nature of mountain campaigns). In many ways, the occupying army resembled the hardened pioneers of North America. They were expected not only to hew timber, but to build homes; not just to occupy the land, but to sow it with seed, to plough and reap it. The tactic was not simply one of self-sufficiency. A love of land was hopefully cultivated within the army, letting the soldier see his fight not as one of aggression but of defence.

The life of the Russian soldier along the Cossack Line, as we know from the tales of Lermontov and Tolstoy, was dull routine. Officers resorted to studying astronomy, performing concerts, or swapping books that had taken over two months to reach them from St Petersburg. The greatest excitement would be gained from horse races, but inevitably these would be won by the Cossacks.

In 1832, when Veliamenov and Rosen launched their Chechen expedition, it can be imagined that it was greeted by the army as a diversion of dubious nature. Still, the foot soldiers would have drawn comfort in their numbers: Veliamenov had gathered nine thousand men and twenty-eight guns. General Tournau accompanied the campaign and left behind a detailed description. His initial fear on crossing the river towards the mountains was the lack of avenues in the forest. There was one route, through the feared Goiten Forest, where Yermolov had cleared the length of a musket shot on either side of the road. But since Yermolov's departure, the forest had recovered, grass, fern and saplings now twined together and rising to shoulder height.

It was a punitive expedition, a redress for the harassing of the

Cossack Line. Nothing but a respite was expected as the reward. From the moment they crossed the Sunzha River they were, according to Tournau, 'engaged in ceaseless fighting'. Every day was the same. Each time the column passed through a forest, it would fall under fire. 'Men fell,' says Tournau, 'but no enemy were seen.' They could hear the crack of the musket, see the puffs of smoke, but never spot the man who had fired. Even during the height of the day, the forests could cast shadows that flickered and moved. Nervous eyes could not settle.

The Chechens never prevented the Russians from taking an *aoul*, nor stopped them from burning their crops. Though the Cossacks (whom the Russians were using as cavalry) would report at the end of each day with several Chechen heads, none of the enemy took quarter, so no information could be gained. Every time a column returned to the Russian camp, its tail would be harassed, Chechens running with howls from the wood, striking a blow, then returning to the safety of the forest. A second column would be sent to relieve the returning one. The monotony of the proceedings and exhaustion began to tell on the Russian troops. Now, every time firewood had to be collected, a battalion was sent out to protect the men. They tried to protect their line by letting pairs of sharpshooters patrol the flanks, but so often were these separated from their column and slaughtered by the Chechens that Veliemenov doubled their number to groups of four. By 1845, the sharpshooters never moved in groups of under twenty.

Veliamenov's men reached the Chechen *aoul* of Ghermentchoug, the richest village in Chechnya at that time. Though Shamil and Ghazi Mullah were in the area, they sent only a small party of their Murids to assist in its defence. The *aoul* was taken by the Russians with little loss of life, the last pocket of resistance contained in three houses at the southern edge of the village. The Russians paused in their fighting and cooked a large dinner of roasted sheep, believing that the remaining combatants would founder in doubt and surrender. The meal was supposed to supply the Russian soldiery with full stomachs and make the Chechens wonder at such confidence, while considering the desperation of their own position.

After moustaches sodden with stew were wiped against cuffs, a field gun was brought out and levelled at the row of houses. So strong was the force of the grape shot that it managed to hit Russian sharpshooters on the far side of the houses. In order to prevent further losses, it was ordered that the three houses should be torched. Veliamenov ordered an old Cossack interpreter to enter the houses, to promise the Chechens not only their lives, but the rights of exchange for other prisoners. In comparison to the subsequent behaviour of both sides throughout the war, this was one of the last noble offers. Tournau reports that after the discussion was concluded, 'a half-naked Chechen, black with soot, came out and made a short speech'. He declared, 'We want no quarter; the only grace we ask of the Russians is to let our families know that we died as we lived, refusing submission to any foreign yoke.'

Under the setting sun, Veliamenov ordered further fires to be set. The Chechens began to sing their death song. Flames rose and in their redness challenged the dying sun. As the song dwindled, one by one the Chechens emerged. The procedure was identical. They would run at the lines of sharpshooters, perhaps clear the circle, only to be bayoneted by the troops behind. Seventy-two men died outside the three houses. The Russians, says Tournau, were sickened by the day's events.

Veliamenov's campaign was effective. Eighty villages submitted to the Tsar, sixty-one were destroyed and the Russians suffered only three hundred wounded. Ghazi Mullah, filled with doubt and knowing that Veliamenov intended his capture, retired to Ghimri and, with Shamil at his side, set about strengthening her defences.

It is impossible to get to Ghimri without undertaking a sharp ascent of five thousand feet, which seemed too precipitous for a modern army. The weather had turned early in 1832, so that by October the mountaintops were thick with snow. Below, there had been no time for harvesting, and grapes hung on the vines. Veliamenov waited for the morning mist to roll down the valley and began the challenge of climbing such a mountain. By means of ropes and ladders, the Russian army gained ground one ledge at a time.

In addition to the formidable natural defence of Ghimri, Shamil and Ghazi Mullah had erected three stone walls, the last of which was connected to a house at either end. The Russians attacked in force, and so quickly that the first two walls of stone were overcome, cutting off any escape from the two houses that had been expected to deliver a lethal crossfire on the Russian troops. Though he could not know it at the time, Veliamenov had, within the stone walls, Ghazi Mullah and Shamil, the architects of the holy war.

From the house where Shamil and his childhood friend stood side by side, they may have been able to see the figure of Hamzad Beg above them. The defence of Ghimri rested on this man, one of the most trusted of the *naibs*. He looked down from his saddle and saw the position of the Russian defences. Making a quick decision that would soon bring about his own rise to the position of Imam, he turned his horse and directed his troops away, leaving Ghimri to the Russians and the pounding of their artillery.

As in Ghermentchoug, no man trapped within the two stone houses asked for quarter. In pairs, they burst from the door, charging towards the line of bayonets that separated them from the safety of the forest. There are two accounts of what happened, neither first hand. Baddeley, by far the most reliable historian of the

Caucasus, says that only two men escaped from the house: the first was Shamil, who, according to Baddeley, broke through the first line of soldiers, wounding three. At the second line, he was bayoneted in the chest, but pushed himself free and cut down his opponent. Stumbling and tumbling down the hill, Shamil made it to the border of the forest, breaking his shoulder and a rib in the process.[8]

Mackie, writing fifty years earlier, in 1856, reports a more prosaic fight. Wounded during his attempted escape, run through the chest and shoulder, Shamil fell to the ground. He was presumed dead and lay there unconscious until dark. The second survivor was unnamed. Ghazi Mullah was dead, identified by returning natives. Shamil, terribly injured, was considered close to death for near on four months. Understandably, Veliamenov reported with pride to Tsar Nicholas. He proclaimed not only the death of Ghazi Mullah, but of Muridism itself.[9]

Hamzad Beg was an *abrek*; though well educated, his career had been distinguished only through perfidy. Until he had encountered Ghazi Mullah at Ghimri he had been a hard-drinking dissolute youth, the son of a wealthy noble. Despite this, none of the other *naibs* questioned his dubious actions at the defence of Ghimri and he was elected as the Second Imam of Dagestan. Shamil was not considered. Presumed dead after the taking of Ghimri, he was being cared for by shepherds who lived even above the *aouls*. A man might walk on the roofs of their houses and not know it, the architect of the abodes being only ice and time, carving follicles with tiny openings into the mountainside.

In a rare clear moment between bouts of delirium, Shamil begged the shepherds to fetch him his wife. With her support, Shamil was transported to his father-in-law's *aoul*, where mixtures of wax, tar and butter were pressed to his wounds. His recovery was slow, but in the last years of his life he would choose this time with his wife as among his happiest days. The peace was interrupted with the arrival of his sister, her chastisements of inaction stinging Shamil. How could he dwell alone on a mountaintop when his people sought his guidance, his strength the core of their resistance? His sister's visit prompted a relapse. According to the superstitions prevalent at the time in Dagestan, Shamil attributed his lapse in health to the fact that his sister had worn jewels on her visit. They were thought to open wounds, to increase sufferings, such was the association of vanity.

Far below Shamil's resting place, Hamzad Beg took as his bodyguard a troop of Polish soldiers, enthusiastic in their hatred of the Tsar. The curtailing of all pleasures continued under Hamzad's nurturing of Muridism. Not only was drinking prohibited, but now music, dancing and marriage feasts were also forbidden. Shamil's miraculous return, six months after the fall of Ghimri, was interpreted as a sign of favour from Allah. Feared dead, Shamil was now a talisman of endurance. As in the days of Ghazi Mullah, he became the favoured *naib*, the most devoted and hardened of the Murids.

However, from his first days it seemed as if Hamzad was motivated not by religious or even nationalist tendencies, but from the desire for personal aggrandizement and revenge. He held a particular grievance against a woman called Pakhou-Beekhi, the greatest khansha of Avaria, who had raised the young Hamzad Beg as her own. After suffering an early defeat in his days fighting under Ghazi Mullah, Hamzad had travelled to Tbilisi, the capital of Georgia, and had volunteered to submit to the Russians in return for a pension. Instead, he had suffered the ignominy of immediate arrest. His release was coordinated by a powerful khan, who had seen the opportunity of using Hamzad Beg as an instrument of revenge against Pakhou-Beekhi (the khan had been spurned when he sought to marry the khansha's daughter). Upon Hamzad's

Ancient watchtowers in northern Georgia

АРТИЛЛЕРИЯ НАИБА ТАЛХИГА У ШАМИЛЯ　　ВЛАДИКАВКАЗ

Shamil's artillery

CAR AND
OCCUPANTS
COOLING DOWN —
THE AUTHOR, TARAN
AND ILYA, WEARING
HIS PAPAKH

HINALIQ, IN THE
'MOUNTAIN OF
LANGUAGES'

BANDIEV KISHI WITH
EVIDENCE OF HIS
GREAT AGE

SHAMIL AND HIS
NAIBS, C. 1850
(HULTON ARCHIVE)

SHAMIL BASAYEV
(REUTERS PHOTO
ARCHIVE)

THE TEAM — (FROM LEFT TO RIGHT) THE AUTHOR, TARAN,
JOHN AND ILYA — ON MOUNT SHAMIL

release, promises were made and kept secret, Pakhou-Beekhi being too powerful a character for a mere *naib* to move against.

During the following two years, Shamil and Hamzad Beg spread the doctrines of Muridism. Pakhou-Beekhi, knowing that all of Avaria, save the capital (her own domain), had now fallen to Shamil and Hamzad Beg, agreed to accept Muridism, but would not submit to joining the Ghazavat against the Russians. As was customary, she sent her youngest son, an eight-year-old, as a hostage for good behaviour. Hamzad invited her two remaining sons to parley a short distance from the capital. Despite bringing twenty bodyguards, the two sons were butchered. When Hamzad hesitated in his treachery, it was Shamil who encouraged him. There was little resistance in the storming of the capital. Pakhou-Beekhi was beheaded, the act witnessed by her surrogate son, Hamzad.

Hamzad was to die shortly afterwards, brought down by a combination of reverberations from his inconstancy and the arch fanaticism of the recently converted. Two brothers, upbraided for their use of tobacco and angered by the treatment of Pakhou-Beekhi, assassinated him as he prayed within his own mosque. Shamil reacted immediately: the brothers were executed and Pakhou-Beekhi's remaining progeny, her eight-year-old son, was strangled, his body thrown from the bridge above Ghimri. Shamil, the Third Imam of Dagestan, was to rule for twenty-seven years. Though his reputation against the Russians was focused on his ability to fight and endure, he was never above brutal pragmatism. The manipulation of tribal politics, coercion, threat and execution were low hurdles to leap so that Shamil could coordinate resistance against the infidel Russians.

# CHAPTER 9

# Heading North

*Our descent from Hinaliq is troubling. We have, in the most ungracious manner, forgotten to bring gifts with us. Our intentions had been good, but had been worth nothing, and all the joy of having been guests evaporated. The sacks of flour and sugar that we were supposed to have bought in Baku had somehow been forgotten and it is only now, when we are ending our stay with Avass, that we realize that the back of the Jeep is empty. In an attempt to make up for such rudeness, when Avass asks if we would like to buy any woollen stockings, we overenthuse. Soon half the village is lining up at Avass's door, each with enough stockings and slippers for a dancing school. Avass selects the women we should buy from and we carry our purchases to the rear of the Jeep. We then try to give Avass some money for our stay, which turns out to be a dreadful offence.*

'I cannot take this money,' he says, staring at the floor. 'If you give me money, then you are not my guests, you will no longer be my friends. Give me money, if you wish, but then never come to my house again. Never walk through my door.'

We apologize profusely and when Avass then asks for a ride in the Jeep down to Quba, we are happy to accept. He emerges from his house packing together the money he has earned from our purchases and dressed in a shiny green suit with winged lapels. It is a remnant of the days of disco fever and could have been worn without shame on Rodeo Drive twenty years ago. It is hard to describe just how incongruous it looks against a backdrop of sheep and mountains. Altogether, we are now eight in the Jeep, crushed together in days of dirt and sweat, each man smoking and ashing over the next. We stop often on the long journey downwards, breaking just to stretch our contorted bodies. Five thousand feet down, Avass pulls out a bottle of vodka and pours everyone a shot. He takes two for himself. He seems to have forgotten the tale of Shamil that he had told us the night before.

Returning to the city of Baku, we begin to plan a second visit to the north. In the past months, back in New York, Taran and I had discussed plans of how to enter the north Caucasus. Shamil moved on the borderlands, it is true, but the scenes of his greatest victory and his most severe defeat lie across the border, in Chechnya and Dagestan respectively. Taran wishes, at the very least, to visit the city of Gounib in Dagestan, where Shamil had met his final defeat. From America, we had followed news clippings of the region, shrugging at each kidnapping, silent when bodies were found.

In Azerbaijan, we investigate, as quietly as is possible, the options for heading across the border. The Ukrainian journalist just shook his head. The American Ambassador said, 'I can get you in and out, but you're on your own on the other side. If you're going to do it, I'd take a dozen soldiers, guns and RPGs.' The Azeri cameraman laughed. 'You take soldiers, you must pay them. Maybe you pay them each a hundred dollars a day. A lot of money, maybe you have eight soldiers. They simple men, you not their blood. You pay them little money, they know they sell you for much money. Do not go.'

If you ask enough men for their advice, you can find a contrarian to agree with you. An American entrepreneur, Jim Philipov, has many friends in Chechnya. He runs a satellite television company in Azerbaijan. His two business partners are young Chechens. They meet with us. We drink beers and they sip tea. We are dirty, T-shirts and muddied trousers; they are decked in Versace blouses and Gucci shoes. There was a third business partner, another Chechen, but he was shot in the head outside of Grozny over a year ago. We decide to be uncustomarily direct. Usually, we have discovered, hours must pass before intentions of business are revealed. After confessing our desires, we are told that if we enter Chechnya, we will be safe under their auspices.

'You will go with us?'

'No. Friends of ours will guide you.'

Then, we play what we consider our trump card, revealing the purpose of our mission: to visit the battle sites of the Murid Wars. Neither of them bats an eyelid, or even acknowledges the name of Shamil with a nod. We might as well have expressed an interest in ornithology. Our foolish hope that we would be greeted as men who wanted to dig past the propaganda towards a new Chechnya is ungrounded. Our confidence was misplaced.

The next day we receive a phone call. Would we like to meet the Chechen Ambassador to Azerbaijan? There is, of course, no such title, as Chechnya is unrecognized throughout the world as a state independent of Russia. Still, Ali Asaev functions in much the same manner, holding similar responsibilities, as an ambassador, and works towards a day his title becomes official. His offices are on the ninth floor of the Aspheron Hotel in downtown Baku, within sight of the Caspian.

Ali Asaev is dressed in a beige Italian suit, a slim silk tie and pressed white shirt. His black hair and beard are cropped close and speckled with grey, the top button of his shirt is undone, the tie pulled down as if he's just arrived back from a day of low sales on the road. A holster peeks from beneath his jacket. We gather in the largest room, the Ambassador flanked by an interpreter and the pair of Versace Chechens. A tray is placed before us, holding tea, beer, sodas, vodka. Everybody chooses tea.

'I would like to show you Chechnya,' begins Asaev. 'I would like to show the world that the Chechens are a good people, very hospitable and not as the Russians portray us. There is a warmth and a depth to the Chechen soul that you will find nowhere else. I am not dismissing the Russians, I am on good terms with many Russians, it is only their Government I despise.'

He pauses to await translation, then continues. 'The Chechens form the heart of the Caucasus. You know, sometimes in the evening, I sit and watch television. I can watch the Discovery Channel, my favourite. I think Chechens are also an endangered species.'

John shoots me a puzzled look.

'Too many people view us as animals,' continues Asaev, 'but we are almost extinct; soon people will realize this. It is only when animals are near to extinction that people take notice. The West has forgotten that if it was not for Chechnya, Russia would still control the Caucasus.'

Maybe so, maybe not. Either way, Asaev is persuasive, at the very least a skilful ambassador. We shift the tack of the interview and ask about Imam Shamil.

'Three-quarters of his soldiers were Chechens,' says Asaev, smiling. 'People forget this. Without the Chechens his fight could not have lasted so long. Many battles in the Murid Wars were fought in Chechnya and nobody there has forgotten. I have the greatest respect for Shamil, he was a true representative of our people.'

'Yet he was an Avar not a Chechen,' I interrupt.

'Which', says Asaev, 'is exactly why he was captured. When the army surrounded him, it was impossible to break through, but a few Chechens managed this. Still, he wished to defend his people until the end. It is the same way we think now.'

'I'm sure you have been told the real reason we are here.'

Asaev opens his palms to us, as if he would like to hear it from our own mouths.

'If we were to enter Chechnya, could you guarantee our safety?'

'If you come as my guest,' says Asaev, nodding, 'I will give you a hundred per cent guarantee, even though a hundred per cent guarantee can only be given in a morgue. Even so, I will ensure that not even one hair of your head will fall on Chechen ground.'

This, naturally enough, made me think of the last Englishmen to enter Chechnya, all of them working for the Chechen Government. Their heads were found on the side of a road. We ask about them.

'They were spies,' says Asaev, shrugging. 'There is evidence.'

Soon Asaev glances at his watch. 'I apologize, but now I must go to meet friends. You are very welcome to join me, but I must hurry. We shall speak tomorrow.'

We thank him kindly and take our leave.

A day later, Ali Asaev calls, true to his word. Preparations for our entrance are being made. Later that afternoon, we are called by his secretary to say that the journey is no longer advisable. The following day, an identical pattern is followed. In the morning, we are green-lighted. Come the evening, the plans are scuttled. Such hesitancy does nothing for morale, fuelling our fears of conspiracies and plotting.

Taran believes that his film will suffer unless he has footage of the north Caucasus and now investigates other paths, including walking over the mountains through Georgia and being smuggled in a car boot across Dagestan. The risk is never alleviated, but Taran comforts himself with the thought that he has already made arrangements with a premier hostage negotiator should things go awry. Even so, he is shaken by the fickleness of the Chechen delegation and finally dismisses the idea as lunatic.

We now focus on Dagestan, equally dangerous. Only two months before, on 22 May, two hundred Muslim gunmen had seized a government building in the capital. They were joined by two thousand supporters in the main square. It could not be considered a revolt, but it had obviously encouraged warlike factions across the border in Chechnya. Like Imam Shamil before them, they still dreamed of a pan-Islamic state stretching from the Black to the Caspian Seas. Russia was quick to see the implications. Yegor Stroyev, the Speaker of the Upper House, said the demonstration could cause a ripple effect: 'It affects not only Dagestan, but places beyond its borders.' The stand-off lasted two days, during which time a pair of Russian policemen were shot and killed. The perpetrators were allowed to walk free from the building, having promised to call off their supporters.

Unlike John and me, pale and blue-eyed, Taran is olive-skinned with dark eyes. Still, he does not look remotely Caucasian, but as another source pointed out, if one of us was to attempt to enter Dagestan, he would be the obvious choice. I am so angry that he would contemplate this that I am tempted to encourage him. Instead, we begin to discuss letting Ilya go. After all, he's dark-skinned, dark-eyed and speaks perfect Russian. In New York, Ilya admitted that he had often played on his resemblance to a Chechen to keep the unwanted at arm's length. This was one of the central reasons for Taran's decision to bring Ilya to the Caucasus.

We set up a meeting with Mr Ramiz's friend and usual employer Vahid Mustafayev. With shaved head, close-fitting Donna Karan wardrobe and muscled body, he looks somewhere between a male model and Hollywood bodyguard. At thirty-two, he runs Azerbaijan's largest independent television company, ANS. He is forthright, extraordinarily generous and a touch neurotic, driven by bursts of energy to leap up, sit down, then break into spontaneous dance moves. His mind spins so fast that occasionally he slams his fist into the table at the inadequacy of his own English, but it is always accompanied by a shake of the head and a smile. He is, his job aside, a celebrity in Baku. Together with his brother, he used to travel around the hottest spots the former Soviet Union could offer, working as a war photographer and cameraman in Afghanistan, Chechnya and Karabagh, the mountainous region that forms the border between Armenia and Azerbaijan. During the war in Karabagh against Armenia, Mr Ramiz and Vahid's brother, Chingiz, joined a unit to capture front-line images. Chingiz was shot and killed. To date, he is the only non-soldier who has been elevated to the position of National Martyr, his name known in every village and *aoul* of Azerbaijan.

Vahid is already responsible for finding us our Jeep and our driver. Now he adds good advice to our list of debts. 'Whatever you are thinking of doing, if you wish to move in the north, you must move as quickly as possible.'

'What's happening?'

'There are always problems, but now, maybe more so. Russian troops build up, Yeltsin speaks loudly. Maybe this means nothing, but since May situation very different. So you should move now.'

Taran is perturbed. Entering Dagestan would make a fitting end to his film. But not only does this come too early in our journey, he also knows that he is responsible for Ilya's life. He is more worried about Ilya's safety than any chronology. Hostages from the former Soviet states are never ransomed for the high sums of Westerners and, with five million dollars in insurance, Taran knows that should Ilya be captured he would also be quickly released. Ilya will still be walking a high wire, but at least there is the semblance of a net.

'You don't go,' Vahid says, pointing at the Westerners. 'You,' he indicates Ilya, 'for you, no problem, I think. For rest, problem guaranteed. In Dagestan, they are killing everyone. They are very cosmopolitan in this way.' Vahid scratches his stubble. 'Is easy for Ilya. I give him cameraman for two days, I give Ilya document saying he is Azerbaijan press. They go in, they out, no problem.'

'Azeris go across the border easily?' Taran asks.

'Many times. The Lezgin people, half of them are in the north of my country, the other half in the south of Dagestan. For press people, only now getting difficult to travel. We had one or two kidnapped, but everything OK at this moment. Maybe not next week.'

'This no problem,' says Ilya. 'In New York, everyone thinking I am Chechen.'

Vahid nods his head in agreement. 'He looks like Caucasus.'

The day we drive north begins nervously. The night before Taran had given Ilya many opportunities to pull out of his mission to Gounib. Ilya explained his position to me: 'You write book, John make photo, Taran film. This I bring to you what you cannot have without me.' He remains calm on the outside, but at four in the morning, when we are preparing to head for the borders, I take a sip of Ilya's tea when he isn't looking. It is heavily laced with whisky.

With a two-day-old son, Mr Ramiz can't have slept. Still, we speed north, tearing past cops waving at us to stop. Mr Ramiz seems to be known well past the parameters of Baku. Many hours later, we arrive in the unofficial capital of the Lezgin nation, Gusari, close to the borders of Dagestan. There's no disguising our foreignness. We stay in the only hotel in town: thin walls, camp-beds, dust balls and dead insects in every room. The fetid bath-room is at the end of the hall; all its windows have been removed for the sake of ventilation but the night is still.

The next morning we drive Ilya to meet a friend of Mr Ramiz who will carry him across the border in a Lada, by far the most common car in the Caucasus. Together with Vahid's cameraman, they give us a quick wave and disappear.

With Ilya gone, the question of his safety hums between us. We are to pass the next two days in the company of Marif, another close friend of Mr Ramiz who happens to live in Gusari. He is a large man, a loose slab of stomach shaded by an enormous handle-bar moustache. He equals Mr Ramiz cigarette for cigarette and sweats only vodka. That first morning he gives us breakfast and a tour of his walled garden. Marif keeps a large bust of Stalin to scare away the birds. He poses beside it for a photograph, know-ing full well that there is a heavy resemblance.

We spend our time investigating surrounding villages and drain-ing the patience of Marif. He takes us along a deep river valley, then pulls his Neva to a stop. He points across the river to a sharp bluff that rises three hundred feet. 'There,' he says, 'that is where Shamil hid after the fall of Akhulgo.'

'Where?'

It takes a full minute for any of us to see whatever Marif is pointing at, but, sure enough, about fifty feet from the crest of the cliff is an opening in the rock. Scraps of grass hang either side of it, a beard to the cliff's mouth. Taran and I are familiar enough with the history and geography of the region to be suspicious of Marif's claims.

# CHAPTER 10

# The Consolidation of Power

*Akhulgo is seen as one of the turning points of Shamil's war against Russia. It was a time of intense conflict, of changing tactics, of questioned commitment out of which grew a determination as hard as rock. In 1837, two years before the fall of Akhulgo, General Fese had mounted another campaign against Avaria, numbering about five thousand bayonets, four hundred Cossacks, as well as artillery. The first stage of the campaign had relied heavily on negotiation and was light on casualties, but after a bloody fight for the* aoul *of Tilitl, six hundred houses strong, Fese made what would prove a small and vital error.*

In three days of fighting, the Russians had managed to occupy the upper part of Tilitl, prompting Shamil to send envoys to sue for peace. The Imam submitted, signed documents of promise and gave up three hostages. General Fese and Shamil suffered a long correspondence, the Russian unhappy with the Avar's choice of words. Shamil would constantly rewrite the letters, but never to Fese's satisfaction.

Shamil's final letter read:

From Shamil and other honourable and learned men of Dagestan. Giving hostages . . . we conclude a peace with the Russian Emperor which none of us will break, on condition, however, that neither side should do the slightest wrong to the other. If either side breaks its promises it will be considered as treacherous, and traitors are held accursed before God and the people.

Such negotiations were purely matters of bluff, pride and immediate occasion. In this case, the only long-term significance of Fese's actions came in their establishment of Shamil as both a civic and religious chief. Once Fese had acknowledged Shamil's importance, the Imam became a figure around which hostile communities might gather. In truth, Fese's position had become remarkably weak; even in surrender, Shamil's was the stronger position. Fese had been drawn deep into Avaria, lost one thousand men, more than half his horses and five of his ten guns. His only option was immediate withdrawal. The pieces of paper he carried, declarations of Shamil's allegiance to the Tsar, enabled him to pen flattering reports of his expedition to St Petersburg. Once again, as far as Tsar Nicholas was concerned, Muridism had been quashed. Instead, all Fese had really achieved was the destruction of several *aouls*, along with their vineyards and crops immediately preceding the harsh Caucasian winter. Unwittingly, he had stoked the fires of hatred and driven the previously uncommitted into Shamil's growing camp.

Having had the largest of his *aouls* reduced to rubble, Shamil spent the latter half of 1837 fortifying Akhulgo. The Russians plainly had little idea of the hatred growing in the mountains. Indeed, the autumn had been chosen as the perfect time for Tsar Nicholas to visit the Caucasus. His generals hoped that his arrival would coincide with a formal submission of the mountain tribes and, to this effect, General Fese was ordered to persuade Shamil down from the crags of Dagestan. In concept, Shamil was to enter Christian Georgia, beg the Tsar's forgiveness for his past sins and provide strong promises of his eternal allegiance to Russia.

Fese entrusted the mission to one of the few generals as well known for his diplomatic success as for his brute strength. One Russian historian declared, 'indomitable courage and extreme energy were too common in those strenuous days to suffice in themselves for any great distinction'. The man whom Fese presumed a breed apart was named Kluke von Klugenau. Immediately, and presumably with little hope in the success of his mission, Klugenau entered the mountains of Dagestan and in short order managed to arrange an interview with Shamil. The general travelled with an escort twenty-five men strong, but on reaching the appointed *aoul* found Shamil had arrived before him with a contingent of two hundred horsemen. Klugenau left his escort behind, and rode alone with his interpreter to an empty knoll that arched between the groups. Klugenau dismounted and, using a crutch that compensated for an ancient wound, leaned and waited. In turn, Shamil advanced with his three closest *naibs*.

They had chosen an impressive stretch of ground to meet upon, a small, broken stretch of turf balanced between a three-thousand-foot drop and a wall of rock of equal height that rose to the west. A *bourka*, the great Caucasian coat that could act as both blanket and tent, was laid on the ground and the general and the Imam sat down to begin their talks.

At first, Klugenau was convinced that he was persuading Shamil. The Imam would praise the general for his eloquence, acknowledge the sense and weight of his opinion, and nod his head in sage understanding. Yet Shamil would concede nothing, repeatedly begging that he could make no decision alone, but would have to consult his *naibs*. Klugenau encouraged the Imam to take the time to consider his requests, and, rising, offered Shamil his hand to shake. Before Shamil could accept the gesture, one of his closest *naibs*, Sourkhai Khan, seized the general's arm and shouted that no infidel had the right to touch the flesh of an Imam. Klugenau shook his arm free, terribly insulted, and raised his crutch to try to knock off Khan's turban, possibly the worst offence that could be committed against a member of the faithful. Shamil grabbed the crutch with one hand and his *naib* with the other, and begged Klugenau to retire immediately. Klugenau was dragged backwards by the interpreter, still spilling the vilest insults a life in the army could provide.

Shamil did consult his allies, as he had promised Klugenau. His answer, which arrived by letter, was most brief. 'From the poor writer of this letter, Shamil, who leaves all things in the hand of God – 28 September 1837. This to inform you that I have finally decided not to go to Tiflis [Tbilisi], even though I were cut in pieces for refusing, for I have oftentimes experienced your treachery and this all men know.' Tsar Nicholas passed through the Caucasus. It was to be another twenty-two years before Shamil would be seen to bow before a tsar.

Baddeley calls this the period of Shamil's 'moral and material' construction, a time for the fortification of Akhulgo and the consolidation of his own authority among the tribes.[10] It did not take long for the news of Shamil's growing influence to filter through the Cossack Line. In early 1839, a decision was reached by the Russians that an attempt should be made on the stronghold of Akhulgo, where the mountaineers might be contained and eradicated.

Nine thousand men met feeble resistance on the way. The problem with besieging *aouls* was that armies, having learned their lessons in previous years, were provisioned lightly to ensure quick movement among the mountains; too often men had died defending wagons containing officers' tents and silver samovars the size of gravestones. The technique and patience involved with laying siege to well-positioned *aouls* were impossible under such haste and yet lines of communication must be kept up, lest an entire expeditionary force be cut off deep in the mountains. This meant that precious time and lives were used building small forts or securing various *aouls* that lay on the road to Akhulgo. Losses were heavy along the way, but only for those who opposed the Russians. On one night of terrible summer rains in the *aoul* of Arguni, an officer named Miloutine, leading a Russian column forwards, made the following report. 'Some [of the inhabitants] were met with the fire of our men and fell, others engaged in hand-to-hand fighting, and were bayoneted, others again tumbled over the cliffs in the darkness and were killed . . . the streets were blocked with corpses.'

Shamil waited as the Russian advancement commanded by General Grabbe closed in on Akhulgo with four thousand men, women and children, one-quarter of whom were men of fighting age. From the beginning of the siege, the Russians could rely on two things. First, the supplies at Akhulgo were limited, and according to the harsh but logical language of tactics, three thousand of the mouths inside were not 'necessary'. Second, the only river close to the *aoul* lay at the foot of one of her two plateaux, a descent of several hundred feet, which made the daily routine of water carrying a dangerous affair.

We already know much of what occurred during the siege: the endless Russian bombardment, the rising stench of Muslim dead, the obliteration of the three Russian columns who advanced too soon upon the *aoul*, met by a combination of falling rocks, sharp-shooters and desperate women and children. Days later, the Russians set about their advance more slowly, often fighting as hard against nature as they were against the Murids. In one case, it had taken an entire company of infantry two months to repair a path that Shamil's men had destroyed. The infantry could only advance after tackles and ladders enabling the scaling of a 140-foot rise had been constructed.

On 5 July Major Tarasevitch arrived at the siege with fresh ammunition for the field guns, which soon resulted in the lower half of Akhulgo being reduced to rubble. Still, every time the infantry made an attempt to storm the walls, they were repelled by the stones from the very houses they had destroyed. The Russian position was not enviable: to retire at this point, with such heavy losses, would have enhanced the cause of Muridism tenfold.

General Grabbe resorted to previously untried subtleties. He feigned the construction of a bridge above the older part of the city. Predictably, the enemy massed its forces opposite the Russian position. Simultaneously, three entire companies were driven across the river beneath Akhulgo, gaining ground on what had previously been Shamil's territory. On either side of the river, the Russians worked feverishly to span the waters with a prefabricated structure. A day later, two battalions crossed the river. Grabbe had secured a fine position to build a new battery. His mortars and guns could now strike deeper into the *aoul*, so that what was already rubble could be reduced to dust. Mid-July until mid-August passed in this way, artillery pounding Akhulgo while the infantry worked mostly as carpenters and workmen, carving and constructing wooden shields that were hung with chains over the most vulnerable paths, making it impossible for the mountaineers to pick off stray Russian soldiers.

By now, in the heat of the summer, conditions had become miserable for both forces. One-third of the Russians had fallen to sickness, wounds or the guns of the Murids. Russian sharpshooters lined the trails that daring Murids passed on the way to take water from the river. Akhulgo was completely surrounded, battered day and night by endless shelling. Unsurprisingly, Shamil lost heart, knowing that the fate of his own family, still gathered about him in the *aoul*, lay in his hands. Though initial attempts at parley had been dismissed by Shamil, on 17 August Grabbe offered him a final opportunity: to turn over his son as a hostage, or Akhulgo would be stormed at morning light.

Jamal al-Din, Shamil's son, did not appear that evening and Grabbe was left no option but to stand by his word and assault Akhulgo. The fighting, after such a long and draining siege, lasted only until noon. The Russian losses were comparatively heavy, but Shamil's exhausted Murids fell under waves of infantry. Numbered among the dead was Sourkhai Khan, the man who had tried to stop Klugenau from shaking hands with Shamil. As Shamil's most important *naib*, controlling all military matters, his death must have shaken the Imam. Raising a white flag, Shamil sent his twelve-year-old son towards the Russians as a hostage.

The Russians withdrew and it seemed as if all that remained would be the unravelling of the details of surrender. During the first negotiation between Shamil and the band of Russian generals, the Imam's conditions – that he and his son should remain in Dagestan – were deemed unacceptable. After three days of parleys Shamil discovered that during the talks the Russians had escorted his son from the mountains. Shamil's spies reported that Jamal al-Din had been taken from the foothills in a carriage and was rumoured to be en route to the Tsar's palace in St Petersburg. Both sides withdrew from talks, Shamil considering the dispatching of his son an unequalled and duplicitous sleight of hand. The order was given by General Grabbe for the assault to continue.

The next Russian attack was met with such unheralded resistance that the Russians immediately retreated. The following morning they attempted to take the *aoul* once more, and met with no resistance whatsoever. The entire *aoul* was busy attempting to escape across the chasm beneath to a smaller, sister village. The artillery trained its guns on the heights while the infantry rushed to cut the mountaineers off from a bridge. More than a thousand bodies were counted, choking the river with blood. Nine hundred more were captured, still others had escaped upwards, into caves higher than the *aoul* itself. The siege was over, leaving three thousand Russians dead or wounded, still more incapacitated from disease. Yet Shamil could not be found.

Knowing that his cause was hopeless, Shamil, with his surviving wife and child, was part of the group who had headed upwards for the caverns. On the night of 22 August, Shamil had led his family quietly down to the river banks. Tying a group of logs together, he had sent his makeshift raft out into the river, empty. As he predicted, it caught the attention of the pickets posted along the river, who pursued the raft, firing across the water. At the same time, pushing his family in front of him, Shamil made his way downstream, along the banks of the river, until they came to a ravine. Presuming he had travelled far enough for safety, Shamil ordered his small party inland, his child now strapped across his back. The group stumbled across the Russian line. Both Shamil and his son were wounded, a Russian officer killed outright in the brief exchange. Still, Shamil hurried his family into the darkness. The Russians, having no officer to give orders, decided not to follow the lone mountaineer and his family. He was, after all, seriously wounded and would most likely die in the rocky wastelands of Dagestan.

It was a true nadir for the Imam. His sister had died at Akhulgo, as had his second wife. He had lost his closest adviser, led thousands to their deaths and given his first-born son to the Russians for nothing at all. Several miles from Akhulgo, he was relieved to recognize men from his home town of Ghimri standing not half a mile away. Knowing that Shamil had been beaten, and with their own *aoul* already conquered by the Russians, these men of Ghimri did not stop to help the Imam; one levelled his gun and fired in Shamil's direction. The Imam cursed them then turned his family away and began to move slowly towards Chechnya.

# CHAPTER 11

# Lying in Wait

*Sleeping habits can be indicative of character. Taran has the power*

*of snatching a rest, grabbing pieces when he needs it. He has an*

*extraordinary ability of falling asleep during dinner, one moment*

*chewing bread, the next head cocked back, frozen and snoring*

*before the mutton arrives. Inevitably, Ilya would wake him by*

*licking his finger and sticking it in the director's ear. John doesn't*

*nap, but once taken by evening sleep is impossible to wake. Even*

*a torch in the eyes and two swift kicks merely elicit a change of*

*position. For Ilya, sleep seems a battle: he spins and slaps and*

*swears at mosquitoes throughout the night, then lies dead to the*

*world at dawn. Taran has acquired the habit of waking him with*

*a glass of water in the face, which inevitably leads to a day of*

*intense resentment. I seem to pass out best in cars, woken either*

*by my head cracking against the glass as Mr Ramiz sends us hurtling into a pot-hole, or else by Ilya sticking pens up my*

*nostrils. It's hard to believe that I miss him.*

Two days before we had been talking together, Ilya trying to make me understand that all the changes in the former Soviet republics that the West heralded with open arms had brought nothing but misery and instability to the majority of inhabitants. 'Before,' he had said, 'I live like king, I have three cars and no problem. Now, I see these countries, and I have been here before. I want to cry, it make me cry. There is too much change. This not coming back, this not yesterday.' Despite these words, Ilya was still fuelled by an enthusiasm. I had asked if he was worried about his journey. He had shrugged and said, 'In Uzbekistan we have say, that he who don't risk, never drink champagne.'

Stretched out on a thin, rusted cot I am reading through Herodotus' reports from the edges of the Greek world. He never entered the Caucasus, but gathered all his information second hand, which led many scholars to believe it was totally unreliable. The mountains, Herodotus wrote, were populated by men with goat's feet. There were many strange tribes, including one that slept through the deep winters, hibernating like bears.

However, Herodotus got a surprising amount right. There may never have been hoards of gold guarded by gigantic griffins, but archaeological discoveries have confirmed some of his previously derided conjectures. There were indeed men from the region who made cups from the heads of their enemies. Archaeologists also discovered quivers made of skin from the forearms of the vanquished and confirmed that celebrations for the dead included entering a miniature tent filled with burning marijuana. My mind, in these late hours, is busy imagining Ilya divided, recycled and celebrated.

At four in the morning, there is banging on the door. Nothing can wake John, but Taran and I stagger to our feet.

Ilya smiles widely as the door opens. 'I'm back.'

'What happened?'

'Problem at border on way in. Seven-hour wait, no problem. Then car break down, tyre go. Man help, we talk of Shamil, we drink together, much drinking, then he leave and come back with more tyre. Then drive to Gounib. No problem.'

Ilya, it turns out, has not only made it to Gounib and back, counting his journey as the most beautiful he has ever taken, but also made friends most miles along the way. He had climbed above the modern village of Gounib, to where the *aoul* once stood before Russian bombardment destroyed it. There, inside a makeshift mosque, he found two small boys praying before a reproduction of Shamil. The branches of the trees that surrounded the low building were tied with thousands of strips of cloth, resembling myriad bandages binding wooden wounds. They are prayer rags, marks of intent, and are found not just outside mosques but also about Christian churches in the Caucasus. Beliefs are strong in the mountains – they run deeper and longer than organized religion; rituals still repeated, if not understood.

On the road back from Gounib, Ilya had found himself faced with a similar wait at the border, a metal belt of cars stretching back for miles. Another eight hours, estimated the driver. Fuelled by vodka and the ominous prospect of having his papers examined, Ilya decided to cut the queue, roaring the Lada past huddled groups of motorists, stooped in morning rain, driving straight up to the border gates. The guard had waved them to a stop with his weapon. He demanded to know who they were and what they thought they were doing.

'I give him fifty dollar,' says Ilya. 'You see his face. He think it birthday twice one year. Border gate coming up, we going through. He waving, like we his daddy. Love you, love you. Is bullshit. Russian soldier, nobody pay him. Is good money, everybody happy.'

Taran raises an early morning toast to Ilya.

Returning to Baku, we finally understand why the Chechen Ambassador had wavered in his decision as to our journey north. There have been troop build-ups on both sides of the Dagestani border, sketchy reports of violence in Muslim villages just miles from Chechnya. The breakaway republic had suffered so greatly in the last war that open provocation of Russia seemed both foolish and unlikely. We did not dismiss the possibility of war, but were grateful that Ilya had already completed his trip to Gounib.

It seems odd, in a region with such a bloody history and facing the sudden prospect of more conflict, that we find ourselves back in a city so closely connected to the Nobel Peace Prize. Before the name Nobel was synonymous with peace, it was more likely to conjure images of dynamite, arms and oil. The youngest Nobel brother, Alfred, invented dynamite, but it was the middle brother, Robert, who was sent to Azerbaijan in 1873 in an attempt to find decently priced walnut to carve into rifle stocks for the Russian army. Fortunately for the Nobels, Robert's arrival coincided with the birth of the Caspian's oil fever. Instead of spending the money on wood, Robert bought a refinery and persuaded his brother Ludwig to move to Baku. Within fifteen years, Baku was supplying half the world's oil and the two brothers had a substantial part of the market.

Though the Nobel fortune was based on blasting caps and explosives, Alfred's shares in his brothers' Baku venture constituted a healthy portion of his wealth. It was, in fact, Ludwig's sudden death that led to the establishment of the Nobel Prizes. A French newspaper caught wind of the demise of one of the famous

Nobel brothers and mistakenly ran an obituary for Alfred, entitled 'The Merchant of Death is Dead'. It is thus easy to see the establishment of the Nobel Prizes as an attempt by Alfred to rewrite his own obituary. Perhaps more strangely, the money that had enabled the family to travel and invest in Azerbaijan was garnered from their father's munitions factory in St Petersburg. Immanuel Nobel had made his own small fortune producing ammunition not only for the Crimean theatre but also for the Russian army, to use in its fight against Shamil.

CHAPTER 12

# Gambits and Guile

*In 1999, the northern Caucasus were still viewed as danger-*
*ous, but battered beyond organization; a very similar state to*
*Russia's assessment of them in the Murid Wars. In the summer*
*of 1842, so little was thought of Shamil's chances of ever re-*
*organizing resistance that no more than thirty pounds of reward*
*was placed on his head. Shamil settled in a small Chechen*
*village, populated by a mixture of natives and his Avar kins-*
*men. His mere survival at Akhulgo was enough to encourage*
*rumours of his deserved fame and wisdom. The progress of*
*Muridism in Chechnya can be marked by the end of that year,*
*when the reward on Shamil's head was multiplied by ten.*

Tsar Nicholas and his generals had had good cause for optimism. All of lower Chechnya fell with barely a fight, and every
Russian demand was met. General Grabbe wrote to the Tsar, 'The
Murid sect has fallen, with all its adherents and followers . . .
in Chechnya no serious unrest, no general uprising, need be

anticipated.' The one factor that neither General Grabbe nor the Tsar had factored into the equation of conquest was the cruelty of their own commanders. General Pullo, in charge of the army in lower Chechnya, had been appointing cooperative locals to positions of authority where they were quick to exploit their fellow men. Soon a rumour spread throughout the country: their current treatment was merely a precursor for Russia's true intentions – to turn the Chechens into peasants and thereby enforce conscription.

Shamil was quick to capitalize on the unhappiness, galloping between villages and spreading the word of Islam. Not only did lower Chechnya rise with Shamil, but reports of his survival and flourishing caused yet another upheaval in his native Dagestan. Once more, the Russians were surprised to have a widespread uprising on their hands. Still, when forces were engaged in the lowlands, the Russian forces were usually victorious.

Shamil's forces may have suffered many small defeats between 1840 and 1842, but the overall effect was one of growing disgust at Russian oppression. Even those who had originally sided with the invaders now thought hard on their position. The most famous of those to cross to Shamil's camp was a man named Hadji Murad, later immortalized in Tolstoy's final novel of the same name. He had fought with the Russians for the last seven years, ever since his kinsmen had struck down the Second Imam, Hamzad Beg.

Late in 1840 Hadji Murad had been denounced by a powerful khan, close to the Russians, accused of spying for Shamil. On this information, Hadji Murad was arrested, his captors ordered to escort him over the mountains to Shura and to kill him should any rescue be attempted. With a guard of forty-five men, Hadji Murad was taken in chains, a rope tied around his middle, held fast by one soldier ahead of him, another behind. It was November and the mountains were already coated in early season snow. At one point, the path narrowed so that the group had to pass in single file. Hadji Murad yanked the rope from the hands of the soldier in front of him and leapt out over the precipice, dragging the second soldier with him. They fell more than a thousand feet, crashing down the side of the mountain, the deep snow cushioning their fall. The soldier struck a rock and was killed outright, but Hadji Murad suffered only a broken leg. All above presumed them both dead, leaving the escapee to crawl through the snows for a day until he stumbled across a sheep farm. From then on, with all the enthusiasm of the recently converted, Hadji Murad was to become Shamil's most trusted commander. He earned the utmost respect with his frequent brash raids on Russian outposts and is credited with the Caucasian technique of reversing the shoes on his horses to deceive those who attempted to track him.

Along with Hadji Murad, Shamil began to devise a system through which he could conduct lightning strikes against any position through the northern Caucasus. Usually, in the days before the Murid Wars, raids organized against fixed posts were very methodical. *Abreks* would gather and spend up to two weeks discussing the details of their plans. Shamil sought to invent a method by which, at a moment's notice, his Murids could gather in one place from a hundred directions.

One out of every ten households in Chechnya was now bound to supply an armed horseman, called a *mourtazek*, to the cause of the holy war. The remaining households in the village were responsible for cultivating the chosen man's land, reaping his crops and keeping his horses healthy. The *mourtazeks* were all dressed in the long robe of the Caucasus, called the *cherkess*, the men in yellow, their superiors in black, all topped in green turbans, the colour of Islam. The remainder of the male population of the *aouls* were encouraged to swear their lives to Shamil if they happened to be called on. In return, they received two bags of flour a month.

Cowardice was marked by a metal tag affixed to the back of a man's outer garment and Shamil's entourage always included an executioner with his long-handled axe. Such organization and imminent threats were no more to the liking of most *aouls* than the practices of the Russians themselves. To punish one instance of betrayal, Shamil gouged out the eyes of the offender, then burned alive eight members of his family in their house. The situation was typical of a land mired in guerrilla war, the native population damned no matter who they supported, caught between the extremes of occupation by foreigners and the unforgiving nature of Shamil's interpretation of the Sharia.

Shamil's new mobile army was the perfect instrument to strike at thinly garrisoned Russian forts, dotted far apart in the turbulent country. With this new system in place, Shamil was able to move an army of ten thousand men over fifty miles of the hardest terrain in little over twenty-four hours. In one such move against the *aoul* of Ountsoukoul, the Russian garrison suffered almost total annihilation to the sum of five hundred men. The only survivors were those who dared to swim the foaming Koisou. The Russians suffered similar losses all over northern Dagestan between the end of summer and the first deep snows, and though they often held out against far superior numbers, over twelve forts fell along with 2,500 men killed and numerous wounded.

Shamil's entire campaign in 1843 had been directed at loosening Russia's grip on northern Dagestan and was run from his new headquarters at Dargo. It was chosen mainly for its inaccessibility: on a map, it looks particularly close to Russian lands, but in reality the forests covering the terrain were at that time so thick that Dargo was considered impregnable, the safest of locations.

This left the Chechens who lived in the plains open to a difficult year, faithful to Shamil, but frequently punished by the Russians. Their cattle were either stolen or killed, their crops destroyed, leaving them with the fear that they might not survive the winter. Since no man dared to entreat the Imam for an exception to be made in their desperate cause, a group of Chechen *aouls* drew lots among their deputies to send a delegation to seek Shamil's permission to sue the Russians for peace. The Chechen deputies armed themselves only with coin, not for Shamil, who would not succumb to bribery, but for the weaker of his followers whose enthusiasm might be kindled by the fire of gold.

Together they decided to strike at the weakest link in Shamil's entourage, his mother, Bahou-Messadou, an elderly woman known as much for her kindness as for her son's devotion to her. Their choice made at least some sense, since Shamil's mother was known to favour a less strident interpretation of the Sharia than the one preached by her son. The Chechen deputies bribed their way to Bahou-Messadou's door and obtained a meeting with the old lady. The same evening, mother visited son. She made the supplication on behalf of the deputies, but was seen to leave in tears. Shamil left his seraglio moments later and silently marched into the mosque.

The matter of surrender, Shamil had declared, was a question that only Allah could decide. Rumours spread throughout Dargo and the population was summoned to the mosque to await Allah's decision. Shamil remained inside for three days and three nights. When, on the third day, the doors were opened, Shamil described the instructions that he had received from above. The Chechen application was shameful. They were aware of their treachery to the extent that they could not even approach the Imam directly, but made their attempt through the weakness of woman, in the person of his own mother. Allah had commanded that the first person who petitioned for submission would be given one hundred lashes. This first person, continued Shamil, was his own mother.

The people who had gathered around the mosque began a wailing that masked Bahou-Messadou's own cries as she fell before her son. Her hands were bound behind her back and a whip brought for Shamil. On the fifth blow that the Imam delivered to his mother she lost consciousness. Shamil knelt and wept beside her. Standing, he announced to the crowd that Allah had also said that the mother's punishment might be allowed to fall upon the son. He removed his red robe, bared his back and demanded that his *naibs* deliver the last ninety-five strokes. Any of his followers who restrained their blows, he added, would be killed. The whip was thick, made of cured hide. After the last blow fell, still conscious, Shamil stood and walked towards the Chechen delegation. His flesh had been cut deeply, the skin separated like pages turned back from a book. The Chechens did not even try to implore mercy, but knelt and pressed their heads to the ground, knowing that a quick death was the most they might hope for. Instead, Shamil ordered them to stand before him, then told them to return to their homes and to tell their people what they had seen and heard.

It was theatre: an emotional, abusive three-day drama, a skilful conflation of tension, surprise and effect. Those Chechens who had doubted the Imam's holiness were now convinced that he was Allah's prophet on earth. The question of submission was not raised again, for only a direct order from Allah could ever persuade a Caucasian to raise a hand deliberately towards his own parents. The story of Shamil's actions wound its way up the mountains, carried in whispers and half-truths from village to village.

At the end of 1843, Tsar Nicholas sent another twenty-six battalions and four regiments of Cossacks to the Caucasus. He wrote that with such an investment, he 'expected corresponding results'. He also wrote that political paths should be explored and money spent turning those closest to the Imam against him. Oddly enough, despite this massive outlay of men and equipment, Tsar Nicholas still referred to Shamil as a brigand. The Tsar believed Shamil and his forces could now be subdued within a year.

In 1845, the command was given that the centre of Shamil's lands must be broached, Shamil himself engaged and defeated. The task was given to a close friend of the Tsar, Prince Vorontsov, a successful commander from the Napoleonic Wars and a wealthy aristocrat. He spoke fluent French and English, his mother being from the Pembrokeshire gentry. His staff was drawn from the greatest families of St Petersburg, all preferring the French language to Russian. They did not pack lightly, but brought tents, furniture and luxury stores, all of which evoked wry smiles from the established Caucasian battalions, well versed in mountain warfare.

Vorontsov arrived in the Caucasus after the snows melted and was immediately caught between the Tsar's wishes for an immediate expedition and the cautionary advice of his own generals. He felt compelled to execute St Petersburg's orders, but obviously with some hesitation. He wrote, 'If God is not pleased to bless us with success we shall nevertheless have done our duty, we shall not be to blame, and we can then turn, somewhat later, to the methodical system which will bear fruit, though of course not so quickly as a victory over Shamil himself.' Five days later, he added in another letter, 'I dare not hope much success from our enterprise.'[11]

The Chechen and Dagestan columns were combined: 21 battalions of infantry, 4 companies of sappers, 46 field guns, 16 *sotnias* of Cossack cavalry and 1,000 native militia on horseback. Baddeley estimates that their total number was not less than eighteen thousand.

Though Shamil's tactics relied on a creative use of geography, such strategy was hardly new. It was a familiar course of action of the great nomadic tribes of the steppe, always employed when dealing with a superior force. Most famously, it was used to defeat the richest man in Rome, Marcus Crassus, when he campaigned against the Parthians in 54 BC south of the Caspian Sea. He knew that with seven legions, four thousand light troops and four thousand cavalry, all he had to do was confront the Parthians in order to defeat them. Plutarch reports that Crassus drove his army into the plains, marching them ceaselessly until finally he believed he had met an enemy sizable enough to engage. He had won small successes along the way, capturing just enough stores that the Parthians had abandoned to persuade him to push on. Only now, though, had he engaged a sizable army.

Like the Chechens, the Parthians preferred to fight from horseback, but the size of the force that confronted Crassus left him in no doubt of his victory. The limited numbers of the enemy enticed the Roman cavalry to charge. They were drawn off several miles, then circled by the Parthians so that a great cloud of dust removed the Romans from sight of their commander. A second division of Parthians now arrived and the Roman cavalry was slaughtered. Crassus' son who had led the charge was unhorsed. His men took him to a low hill, where, realizing their situation, they fell on their own swords. All the while the main force of the Romans was harried by archers on horseback. A disheartened Crassus then put his faith in a traitor who led their supposed retreat in dizzy circles until his own officers persuaded Crassus to sue for peace. During the negotiations, Crassus and his entire delegation were murdered and the remnants of the army taken prisoner. The close-fighting

Roman army had been soundly defeated without ever truly being engaged. However, the Caucasian population, unlike the Parthian, was not nomadic. Most of the suffering of this partisan war fell not on the mobile groups of soldiers, but on the sedentary natives who refused to abandon their *aouls*.

As with the Parthians before him, Shamil had no plans to confront his enemy directly, leastways not on their outward march. Knowing that the further from their forts he enticed them the heavier their losses would be, Shamil presumed that their ultimate objective would be Dargo. It remained his best-armed stronghold, reachable only through the thickest forests and mountain passes. It was an objective that both sides were more than happy with.

For the first twenty miles of their slow journey, the Russians met with little opposition, driving their carts, carriages and guns through mountain passes and by abandoned *aouls*. Though it was the first week of June, the weather turned unexpectedly, sudden winds at eight thousand feet bringing frost and snow that killed almost five hundred horses. The next month brought nothing but slow progress, the Russian column stretching for miles in the most awkward terrain. The *aouls* they encountered had been burned before their arrival. In a letter dated 9 July 1845, the Tsar wrote to Vorontsov, 'God has crowned you and your heroic troops with deserved success.' Vorontsov knew better. Already, he realized that he was too far from any Russian base to build himself a defensible fort. The men were on short rations and their line was now strung out, marking their progress like fairy-tale pebbles scattered through a forest to ensure their way back.

Extraordinarily enough, despite his worries, Vorontsov had progressed to within ten miles of Dargo, with minimal casualties. It took three weeks for the provision train to reach the line but supplies were already limited. Foraging raids of the surrounding area showed only the desperation of their situation. Shamil had ensured that every sheep and goat had been flushed from the area, every vine and vegetable uprooted. The July sun had scorched the grasses, making them inedible for the horses. Vorontsov was faced with a difficult choice. Finally he elected that he must push on before his army became even weaker. Vorontsov would, when necessary, direct a part of his force back towards the oncoming train of provisions when news of their imminent arrival reached him.

The first column to move towards Dargo, now only five miles distant, found that their only path of descent was blocked every quarter-mile by fallen trees, thick-trunked and heavy with branches. They crossed the first obstacle, then the second. The eager front of the column, in its rush towards glory, was now separated from its fellows. The area between the fallen branches was suddenly filled by Chechens, rushing from the bunched undergrowth either side of the path. Initial losses were heavy, including a group of officers and one general. As soon as Vorontsov deployed the native militia into the woods, the enemy melted away and the head of the column was free to proceed to within a mile of Dargo, where they waited for the general's staff to catch up. Beneath them, Dargo was in flames, fired by the Murids. The Russian objective had been achieved without direct confrontation, yet they could not hold it so far from Russian-controlled territory, even without the customary snows that would make the return march impossible within three months. There were now twenty-seven miles between their current position and safety. Vorontsov waited patiently for his provisions to arrive.

On the high banks of the river above Dargo, Shamil gathered his men. Though they discharged their guns in the direction of the Russian camp, it was as much a gesture of avoidance as aggression. Much more aggravating to the Russian columns was the presence in Shamil's camps of several hundred deserters, who, while Vorontsov awaited his provisions, insisted on playing Russian military marches throughout the day, filling the blackened *aoul* with their mocking strains. In order to dismiss both the shot landing in his camp and the presence of the deserters, Vorontsov ordered an expedition up the bluff to attempt to capture the guns.

The bulk of the column watched as their brethren walked through a field of waist-high maize then scaled the heights of the bluff. It was a complete success: all four guns were captured. Yet, on their return, in plain view of their column, the Russian force was attacked from neighbouring woods as they passed back through the field of maize. One hundred and eighty-seven were killed or wounded. The dead were buried that evening, accompanied by volleys of shot, fired in their honour. In retrospect, it was simply a waste of ammunition. From then on, the dead would be buried in silence. There was, however, some good news. On 9 July a rocket lit the sky above the forest, signalling that provisions had arrived. All that was necessary was for an expedition to be sent to escort the provisions to Dargo. Four thousand men were chosen for the job, a mixture of units, an unusual occurrence, but thought fair since both the provisions and the danger should be equally shared. This return journey, totalling no more than nine miles, would become one of the lowest points of Russian military history, known simply as the 'Biscuit Expedition'.

Once more, as they were forced to recross the fallen trees that blocked the path, the head of the column became separated from the body, and the tail lagged behind them both. Once again, the Chechens occupied the space between the three groups and a day of chaos and bloodshed began. Only at nightfall, when the expedition reached the supply carts, did the fighting cease. Just before sundown the Chechens had captured the coffin of the dead general and in front of the Russians had prised open the lid and thrown the body down a ravine. General Klugenau, in charge of this expedition, should have held his direction and continued south through Dagestan. Instead, he decided to cross the fallen beech trees once more. This time it would be even more difficult. Not only was a hard rain now falling, but he was responsible for cumbersome supplies and a heavy number of wounded.

The first barricade of trees that they reached on their return towards Dargo had been reinforced with Russian dead. The bodies had been stripped, many having given up their hands or heads to trophy hunters. As soon as the first men to arrive began to remove the bodies, they were shot at from either side of the path. An entire group of sappers was slaughtered. Disorder ruled, the van of the column gathering in small groups of twos and threes, fighting their way slowly forwards. The rear of the column had run out of ammunition. They formed a square and waited for their end.

Fortunately for this rearguard, made up of men of the seasoned Karbada regiment, Vorontsov had guessed at their desperation and ordered the remainder of the same regiment to their rescue. Though now entirely separated from the body of the column retreating towards Dargo, the reinforcements, walking over the bodies of their dead, managed to reach their comrades, together fighting their way backwards. Among the bodies the Karbada regiment managed to retrieve was that of a second dead general, which they dragged behind them in a sheet of bark. As darkness fell, their pace quickened and this second body was also lost over the side of a ravine. Nobody tarried to reclaim it. In two days, 556 men were killed, including the two generals. In addition eight hundred were wounded and three field guns lost.

General Freitag, stationed in Grozny, was their only chance. Five messengers were sent through the forest with the information that Vorontsov was now changing direction and heading for Gherzel, rather than making his way back through the forest again. Freitag had written a letter of advice to Vorontsov before the expedition to Dargo had begun: 'On the downward march you will meet in the forest such difficulties and such opposition as . . . you do not anticipate. I feel sure that your Excellency will win through, but the losses will be enormous. However successful your movements, they will have no influence on the subjugation of Chechnya.'

It was a question of belief overriding experience. The faith that Vorontsov displayed in his own men, in their determination and bravery, was fully justified. Yet it meant nothing in the forests and the mountains. Freitag, an old Caucasian hand, could feel only a strange mixture of pity for his commander and gratitude that it was not his own men attempting to take Dargo. Still, Vorontsov could not afford to wait to be rescued. He began to march slowly towards Gherzel, now weighed down by a total of over a thousand wounded men. On the first day they travelled less than three miles.

A painfully familiar pattern was followed on 16 July. Once again, the van of the column rushed ahead, driven by the thought that the safety of Gherzel was no more than two days away. Subsequently, the column was broken, sappers abandoned by heedless troops, men slaughtered by steel and gun, the wounded dispatched by *kindjals*. In one day, there were five hundred casualties, including over a hundred dead. The exhaustion, four days from Dargo, must have been complete. Now, with over two thousand wounded, there were barely enough men to carry their injured comrades, let alone fight the enemy. Vorontsov called an end to his march, closed his column and decided to wait for Freitag. By now, there were no provisions left, the men were not only dispirited, but starving, some resorting to eating maize pulled from the stalks in the fields.

By 18 July, the troops had less than fifty rounds per man left, their encampment subject to constant sniping and occasional sortie. At sunset came the sound of rocket and cannon. Finally, Freitag had arrived. By 20 July the expedition reached Gherzel. Vorontsov had lost 3,433 men. The Karbada regiment, which had fought its way along the line and carried the rearguard on at least two occasions, had lost three-quarters of its 850 men. Vorontsov wrote to the Tsar: 'The Mountaineers have now learned that we can reach them in places hitherto deemed inaccessible.'

# CHAPTER 13

# Staggered Borders and Soft Lands

*It is a long journey from Baku into Georgia, compounded by a staggered border where each checkpoint attempts to exact a bribe of one kind or another. Most trading in the region is informal, farmers packing their tiny cars with their goods. Trunks, seats and floors are crammed with merchandise, often fruit. Now, at the height of the summer, cars are bursting with watermelons. Their axles grind, suspension long gone, their metal bellies scrape against the mixture of dirt and tarmac. Coming across the borders these cars are stopped beside us. Voices are raised, watermelons passed reluctantly out of the windows, cars waved on.*

Save for the mountains in the north, Georgia is a land rich in green hills, leading to the shores of the Black Sea, where the subtropics encroach with a scattering of palm trees and whispers of sand. It was not a country that formed a natural defence to much of anything, finding itself sitting uncomfortably between the Roman and Persian empires, pulled between its Christian origins and the destructive forces of invading Islam. Such continued stretching left Georgia splintered, a series of states and kingdoms that were frequently divided among conquerors, from Tamerlane to the Persian Shah Abbas. By the end of the eighteenth century, the Russian and Ottoman empires were in periods of expansion and Georgia, poised between them, in an especially uncomfortable position. The mad Russian Tsar, Paul I, ignored his predecessor's promises of assistance to their Christian brethren, leaving an indefensible Tbilisi to be razed to the ground by the Turks. It was not until Alexander gained the throne in 1801 that Georgia was rejoined with Russia and her capital rebuilt. Tbilisi was, if not a Russian city, certainly a Christian one, sprinkled with churches, including some that had survived a turbulent thousand years.

Over three thousand years ago, Jason landed on the Georgian coast, in search of the Golden Fleece. There were many golden fleeces about: sheepskins weighed down with rocks and left in river beds to catch particles of passing gold. In the years between Jason's departure and the emergence of Georgia as a republic, in 1991, there is only one name that has emerged as familiar as that of the Argonauts. Stalin was born in the town of Gori, which now plays host to a museum bent on nothing short of deification. Once a year, in the middle of the night, it was the custom in Gori for every blacksmith to hammer on his anvil. The Caucasian Prometheus was named Amiran, but he was not so benevolent as his Greek counterpart and instead was intent on mankind's destruction. The annual cacophony of blacksmiths represented a symbolic testing of his chains, to ensure that he would never escape from an eternity of incarceration within the mountains. It is easy to view Stalin's birth in this, of all Georgian towns, as the unleashing of a terror throughout the Caucasus and all of Russia, but you would be hard pressed to find a Georgian who would agree. A sanctification has occurred and the hagiography contains only records of the good days of plenty.

There is no mention of the millions who died in Stalin's purges, all the more surprising when one considers how heavily the native son made his homeland pay during the Soviet regime. Beria, Stalin's dreaded head of the NKVD, was also an ethnic Georgian. The liqui dation of entire villages in the Caucasus was politely referred to in letters between the two men as 'the successful fulfilment of state tasks'.

Yet not long after Stalin's death and Beria's subsequent execution, Khrushchev denounced Stalinist excesses — only to find a large demonstration formed in Tbilisi to protest Stalin's posthumous treatment. It was quickly crushed by the Soviet army, and dozens died. Ilya, as an Uzbek raised in Soviet Tashkent, has no such reservations. In Stalin's museum in Gori he walks straight up to a bronze bust of Joseph Stalin and gives it a loud, open-handed slap. 'Ten years ago,' he says, laughing, 'they would have killed me.'

We have nowhere to live in Tbilisi, only one possible contact, the cousin of a taxi driver Ilya had befriended in Baku. Together, they had bonded buying sheep, gutting and dividing them. Ilya would raise the trachea of the carcass to his mouth and blow, the lung puffing up like a balloon. Then he would breathe in and out quickly to make the lung expand and contract. 'Sheep is jogging,' he would say.

Tbilisi has a beauty and formality that make it seem both regimented and more gentlemanly in comparison to Baku. The Kura River winds through the middle of the city. Churches stand on her high banks, bridges have balustrades, iron-cased balconies lean out from buildings, stretching for river views. There are more than enough Soviet structures to jar the mind from kingdoms lost and treasured queens, but Tbilisi seems reasonably unmarked for a city that was the epicentre of its country's bloody revolution less than a decade ago.

On the far side of the city, sitting above the capital on a steep and dusty hill, is a network of unnamed streets that resemble the layered labyrinths of a Moroccan casbah. A small boy seems to recognize the name of the man we are looking for and climbs into the front seat to guide us. Along an alley, past the black dog and the rooster, through a courtyard, by the children, up four steps and away from the dipped eyes of surprised women. Over a concrete slab where an old man sits with broken glasses balanced on the end of his nose and up twenty steps. This is Lado's house and though we do not yet know it, it will be our base for a month in Georgia.

Within the week, we have been absorbed by the family. We live in two connecting rooms. Lado has moved his family in with his brother, twenty steps beneath us, but the truth is there are no divisions. Sometimes, when we return at night, there are babies asleep in our beds, or else the family has gathered at midnight, all fourteen in the room we have rented. Notions of privacy must be discarded, or else offence would scratch at sanity.

The extended family is devoted to the oldest son, Mahir, Georgia's brightest hope in middleweight boxing. Swinging on the concrete porch is an ancient punchbag, pocked by well-stitched holes. Whenever it is hit hard, it coughs up a cloud of sawdust. Every night, we drink with the men of the family and, with Ilya interpreting, talk of either Muhammad Ali or Imam Shamil. The favoured drink is called *chacha*, a toxic distillation of grape that we buy straight from the back of a factory. It is pumped through a hose into whatever plastic container you choose to bring along. Four or five shots unravel cultural ties, and soon the two brothers are teaching us the fundamentals of boxing.

At fifty, Lado's hands are marked by broken fingers, poorly set so that they can barely bend to make a fist. He has bright, smiling eyes and is forever clapping you on the back or kissing your cheeks.

His brother Baklul is more reserved, preferring to sit apart for the early drinking, then slowly merging into the group. Baklul has the profile of an arrowhead, which gives off the impression of a determined, aggressive man. He has spent the last sixteen years imprisoned for murder. His boxing skills give evidence. While Lado dances, jabbing and ducking, weaving and cutting, Baklul pushes immediately into his opponent, getting close enough to dole out immediate punishment.

No women attend these nightly conferences. Wives and daughters are at the bottom of the stairs, standing by a tap that runs all day and night. They wash clothes, scrub pots, calling up orders to the husbands and fathers above. Occasionally the stooped patriarch of the family emerges from below to join us. He puts both his hands in the small of his back, groans and always begins the same conversation about the good old days of Joseph Stalin. Ilya interprets, laughs and winks at us.

During the daytime, we are either interviewing academics and politicians or preparing journeys into northern Georgia. So much time together has made the group fairly combustible. Every single meal is taken with the same companions and tempers fray, but never explode. It takes little encouragement from our hosts to set up fights between the members of the group. Taran is first up to fight. Boxing gloves appear from unknown quarters. Advice is offered in Russian, Azeri and Georgian. His opponent is John, by far the calmest of the group, always retaining a jovial serenity. His demeanour is at odds with his countenance – the shaved head and bristling goatee. It is the shortest round of boxing I have ever seen. Fuelled by a last shot of *chacha*, one right hook from John leaves the director of the film lying on his back on the hot concrete. Taran tries to rise but wobbles and remains down. Lado and his brother, Ilya and I cannot stop laughing.

So much flexing has gone on over the last month, so much pushing of boundaries and verbal assaults, that now, for the first time, direct confrontation is encouraged. I am sitting watching my stunned friend trying to stop the spinning and I am crying with laughter. None of us knows how to box. Despite our daily lessons, there is no skill, guile or tactics employed. One man simply knocks over another, while both flail.

The sole reason for all this bravado is that there are never any women present. You can say things among men and not be challenged, not have the truth flapped in your face, not have your posturing immediately betrayed by a scornful wife. In short, you can get away with whatever your companions let you get away with. It isn't simple chauvinism, but a constant performance of being male. Taran rises from the concrete, laughing and shaking his head to dismiss the stars. Everyone claps him on the back and offers to share another drink. We sit outside in the night heat for hours. Once again, the electricity in the neighbourhood has failed. It is too hot to move, too hot to sleep. We stare at a pair of cats patrolling the interlocking rooftops.

# CHAPTER 14

# Titled Characters

*On 28 March 1847 a blazing meteor passed over the* aoul *of Dargo. Shamil stood beneath and watched it tear across the sky. The same evening, the outskirts of the* aoul, *populated only by Russian deserters, burned to the ground. It was not a difficult omen for Shamil to interpret. After three months of inaction, Allah was not only calling for a return to battle, but predicting the fate of all Russians who would stand in their way. By the end of the year, a pattern had been established: the Russians would advance, with the goal of a particular* aoul; *a siege would ensue, normally incurring heavy losses for both sides; the Russians would take the* aoul, *but realize that lines of communication could not be kept open; they would retreat, harassed all the way to the plains.*

This was, then, not the aggressive action that Shamil had predicted in the meteor passing over his mountains, but a drawn-out stalemate that consumed both money and men. Russia's inability to concentrate her forces on the Caucasus was now exacerbated by her wars against Turkey in 1853 and France and Britain in the Crimea in 1854. Only a hastily arranged convention in Tehran, where old war indemnities were conveniently excused, ensured that Persia would not stretch the Russian military machine any further. Had the Shah joined his Muslim brothers in the fight against the expanding Russian empire, the Tsar's position in the Caucasus would, most likely, have crumbled.

Instead, with the bulk of Russia's forces now spread on the far side of the Black Sea, more useful employment than the bombardment of *aouls* occurred. The first tunnel in all of Russia was hewn in the Caucasus, roads were built and lines of communication between Russian forts, Tbilisi and Shura much improved. Such constant toing and froing meant that the native population, always subject to the alternating tides of Russian ebb and Murid flow, found their positions untenable. By the early 1850s, the villages occupying this contended strip were forced to decide where their loyalties lay. All were uprooted, some populations heading deeper into Chechnya and others behind the Russian lines. In the end, the advantage fell to the Russians, the empty territory proving much less troublesome than in the previous years of uncertain loyalty and frequent guerrilla raids. Russian success, after all, was measured in the acquisition of territory, irrespective of whether it was populated.

In 1851, a young junker reached the mountains. This was the term given to those who volunteered for service in the ranks of the Tsar's armies, despite noble births and family connections. The stretch of abandoned land that now separated the Cossack Line from the highland Chechens struck twenty-three-year-old Leo Tolstoy:

[The Terek] which separates the Cossacks from the mountaineers still flows turbid and rapid though already broad
and smooth, always depositing greyish sand on its low reedy
right bank . . . no one lives there now, and one only sees
the tracks of the deer, the wolves, the hares, and the pheas-
ants, who have learned to love these places.

In his first letter back to his brother, Tolstoy also mentioned one
of the greatest thorns in Russia's side, Hadji Murad, the Avar noble-
man who had thrown himself from a snowy clifftop in order to
escape the Russians. Tolstoy told his brother that he was now considered 'the finest warrior and horseman in all Chechnya'.

Within two months of Tolstoy's arrival in the Caucasus, he had
good reason to sympathize with the Chechens. He had reached the
area not wrapped in notions of patriotism or driven by the need
for adventure, but directed there by his family, who had recently
had to remove one village from his estate to cover gambling debts
of over sixteen thousand roubles. He had found inveterate gamblers
in the salons of St Petersburg, and now, in the shadows of the
mountains, he once again gave way to his most prominent vice.
Gambling one night, he had fallen so far in debt that he had spent
the night in panic, relating in one letter that he had prayed to 'God,
to get me out of such a disagreeable scrape'. On waking the next
morning, he was given an envelope. Inside were his promissory
notes from the night before. They had been won back from a
Russian officer by a local Chechen friendly to the Russian cause,
named Sado. Thirty years later, Tolstoy would borrow his name to
bestow upon a minor character in what many consider the finest
of his short works, *Hadji Murad*.

Tolstoy understood how rare a connection between a Russian
soldier and a Cossack was, let alone between a titled aristocrat and

the predominantly hostile Chechens. He wrote, 'A Cossack is inclined to hate less the hillsman who maybe has killed his brother, than the soldier quartered on him to defend his village, but who has defiled his hut with tobacco-smoke.' It was the Russian officer who was viewed as the true intruder. The Cossack Line had existed before the conquest of the Caucasus began in earnest. There had been much trading, even intermarriage, between the Cossacks and the Chechens. They shared a love of horses, of weaponry and of land, and though blood was often shed between them, there was a mutual respect that was never extended to the Russian infantry, her officers, or their modes of war.

When Tolstoy did participate in fighting, he confided to his diary in January 1853 that such conflict was so 'ugly and unjust that anybody who wages it has to stifle the voice of his conscience'. It was an issue that troubled him for the rest of his life, but also one that evoked a strong understanding of how the mountaineers must have come to feel about the invaders after less than forty years of war. In *Hadji Murad*, the Russian officer Butler helps lead a column against an undefended *aoul*. It is burned to the ground, all the animals slaughtered or seized and a young boy bayoneted through the back. The following day, the remaining villagers gather to begin to rebuild their village, starting with the mosque. Tolstoy wrote:

> It was not hatred, because they did not regard those Russian dogs as human beings; but it was such repulsion, disgust and perplexity at the senseless cruelty of these creatures, that the desire to exterminate them – like the desire to exterminate rats, poisonous spiders, or wolves – was as natural an instinct as that of self-preservation.

Tolstoy's days in the Caucasus were, for the most part, dull and the source of frequent complaints in his letters. Life was confined. In his station there were 'three shops where drapery, sunflower and pumpkin seeds, locust beans and gingerbreads are sold'. There were also drinking, cards and conversations, most built on rumours of Russian generals and the leading Murids who faced them.

Everywhere that Tolstoy went, one name rang in his ears as often as Shamil's. The Imam had elected to send Hadji Murad to the coastal provinces of the Caspian to attempt to stir their populations against the Russians. While Shamil had now proved himself a tactician, Hadji Murad's activities show him as a man driven more by adrenalin than by religious fervour or a thirst for freedom from the Russian yoke. His body of five hundred horsemen caused much confusion in the provinces now peacefully subjugated by the Russians. In July 1851, wrapped in his deep red robes, Hadji Murad pushed his men over a hundred miles in less than thirty hours, an extraordinary feat in such country. He raided the prosperous *aoul* of Bouinakh, close to Derbent, capturing the wives and children of the Khan, who were later ransomed by Shamil for a large sum of silver.

Yet Hadji Murad's position was unenviable. Having already sided with the Russians once, his own dealings with the khans and chieftains of the region constituted explosive politics. It was, after all, Hadji Murad's kinsmen who had murdered the Second Imam in his mosque. During his lieutenant's absences, Shamil's ear was often bent to continuing accusations designed to increase any jealousy the Imam might have of Hadji Murad's popularity. Above all things, it was a question of succession, Shamil perceiving that Hadji Murad might try to usurp the intended heir, Shamil's own son, Ghazi Muhammed. The first three Imams of Dagestan were not descended from the same line, but were chosen for their supposed abilities. In keeping with the pattern, Hadji Murad would have made a very likely successor. Jamal al-Din, Shamil's oldest son, had been taken by the Russians twelve years before. He was remembered daily by his father, but no hostages of equal importance had ever been found to commence bargaining with St Petersburg.

Though Hadji Murad turned coat on a previous occasion, it is still difficult to see such a man as a traitor. His motivations were not those of greed, or aggrandizement, but of political manoeuvring by which he might keep his life. He was, however, driven by revenge, founded on a blood feud with Akhmet Khan, chief of a prosperous *aoul*. Such influential enemies always guaranteed a tricky progress through the rocky and shifting ground of tribal politics, and it was not surprising that in such a bitter feud both Hadji Murad and Akhmet Khan had at different times sought favour with Shamil *and* the Russians.

With Shamil's proclamation of his own son's inheritance, Hadji Murad must have sensed the tide turning against him. Shamil gathered a cabal and condemned his finest lieutenant to death. The information leaked, Hadji Murad was alerted and without hesitation he turned himself over to the closest Russian fort, which, in turn, immediately sent this prized captive to Tbilisi, many miles from the mountains.

Gone were his armies, his *aoul*, his khanates, his followers and his enemies. He was given a horse and carriage, an interpreter and an aide and was paraded through dinner parties and dances. Tolstoy described Tbilisi in 1852 as a 'civilized town which apes St Petersburg a lot and almost succeeds in imitating it'. Its suburbs were 'very pretty and surrounded by vineyards'. As both a mountaineer and a devout Muslim, Hadji Murad can only have been horrified at the sybaritic comforts of the city, with its marble hallways, women rude enough to address him, wine poured and drunk before him. All that he wished for, all that he had come for, was to change his allegiances, not his mode of life. He desired to fight, no longer against the Russians, nor even Akhmet Khan, but against Shamil.

In letters to his viceroy, Prince Vorontsov, Tsar Nicholas preached caution. He reminded Vorontsov that Hadji Murad was a man who had thrown himself from a mountain precipice in an effort to escape the Russians. Nor could the Tsar be ignorant of how his men had previously treated Hadji Murad. They had not only bound his arms behind him and marched him through the mountains, but had also once chained him to the wheels of a cannon in a public square. Could a man forget such humiliations?

The decision was taken by Vorontsov not to provide arms to Hadji Murad's faithful followers, despite his entreaties at least to leave Tbilisi long enough to take his wife and children away from Shamil's lands. Hadji Murad's daily demands were treated with diplomatic havering, promises always made for the next day, interpreters begging for his patience with their Russian customs. His only solace was to be found in the company of the five Murids who were allowed to escort him about Tbilisi, their party always accompanied by a guard of Cossacks.

He knew by now that his family had been imprisoned in Shamil's own stronghold at Dargo, and also that the Imam had promised not death, but unimaginable torture to Hadji Murad's son should any attempt at rescue be made. It would be hard for anyone to listen to such news and not tug at their chains, but for a man who had ridden against larger foes, raided well-defended positions, even sneaked so far behind Russian lines that he interrupted a formal dinner party, the answer was now simple.

Hadji Murad sent word that he would like to take his daily ride. His five Murids accompanied him and they, in turn, were escorted by a small guard of five Cossacks. Once outside the Muslim enclave of Nukha they spurred their horses and attempted to outrun their captors. The Cossacks had been provisioned with finer horses and soon drew near. Their captain called out for Hadji Murad to stop. He did, and promptly shot the approaching captain through the heart. The Murids charged the stunned Cossacks, killing three and sending the remaining man running back to his commanding officer. Some peasants who had witnessed the scene alerted the colonel of the closest garrison, who gathered a large group of men and set out at once, hoping to catch the escapees in the foothills, before they could ford the river and head upwards, into the mountains.

In the early morning mists, Hadji Murad and his five companions misjudged their route and found their horses up to their fetlocks in the cloying mud of a flooded rice field. By the time they had extracted themselves, all advantage had been lost and the sun was bright above them. Deciding to wait until dark in a thick copse, they failed to realize that an old man had spotted them while they sought their hiding place. Their position had been reported to the colonel.

The copse was surrounded. Knowing that Hadji Murad could have little more ammunition than that which he had stripped from the dead Cossacks, the colonel cautiously drew shots from the wood by advancing his men in a slow and deliberate manner. Slicing the throats of their mounts, the six Murids made a bulwark of horseflesh and picked off the boldest of their enemies as they approached. By now the news of Hadji Murad's escape and imminent capture had spread through the surrounding villages and many rode out of the hills either to participate in or simply observe his capture. One who came to watch was none other than the son of his oldest enemy, also called Akhmet Khan. All offers of quarter proffered by the Russians and his fellow mountaineers were refused by Hadji Murad.

Five hundred men had now gathered and they closed in on the copse, pushing aside the undergrowth, not knowing for sure if Hadji Murad had any ammunition left. The answer came in the death chant, the six surrounded men singing their final song, their cartridges almost exhausted. They drew their swords and charged their enemy. Hadji Murad was shot twice. He leaned against a tree and managed to stuff his wounds with cotton, hoping to slow the flow of blood. Dispatching the first to come at him with the last shot of his pistol, he pushed himself upright and was sent reeling by several shots. He lay on the ground, staring upwards at the branches stretched towards the sky. Those who reached his body first waited for Akhmet Khan, who drew his *kindjal* and severed his enemy's head.

His body is buried on the path to Mount Shamil. It is a quiet grave, a yard or two from thick foliage. It may not be the copse where he made his final stand, but it would have been dense enough to hide six horses and six men. You can't help but think you see shaded figures pass between the trees. Hadji Murad's head was taken to Vorontsov, who put it on display in Tbilisi for the public. Later it was embalmed as a gift for the Tsar.

CHAPTER 15

# Georgian Nights

*Our car survived last night though our host's did not. Retiring*
*by midnight, we had heard the screams, the fighting beneath,*
*but our enquiries were waved away with smiles. Whatever was*
*going on was considered private, probably embarrassing and*
*absolutely none of our business. Only this morning did we piece*
*together the events of the night. Our host's cousin, who had*
*drunk with us the night before, had never returned home, but*
*managed to drink until dawn. Nor did he stop, but continued*
*straight through the day into darkness, returning to an angry*
*wife who had screamed at him so loudly that the family gath-*
*ered round. Wife faced husband and wagged her finger in his*
*face, husband raised his hand and his brother intervened. The*
*two brothers began to fight, fell together out of the door into*
*the narrow alley where cars were parked against the walls of*
*houses. Knives were drawn and while one raised his weapon, the*

*other ducked, the blade missing his head, slicing deep into his*

*arm, and down through the bonnet of our host's car. If in fury*

*it had passed so smoothly through metal, there was no doubt it*

*was a murderous blow. The brother was sleeping now, the money*

*for the week long since spent on vodka and* chacha.

It made me think of the rising tensions amid our own group. Ramiz and Ilya had little patience for one another now, Ramiz insisting that Ilya was a lunatic, Ilya that Ramiz was a fool. They had then begun to deride one another's parents, a taboo Caucasian subject, until they were separated. I am also realizing that Taran's need for control has begun to aggravate me. The smallest things make me bristle: the order in which tea is served, who sits in the front of the car. I perceive subconscious slights in all his actions.

Waking this morning my jaw had ached, still sore from a right hook from John last night. He can't smile back, because his lip is too badly split, but we manage to agree without words that we are a pair of fools. It had started at a circumcision party. Four hundred people had gathered to celebrate an absence of foreskin. An hour earlier, the four-year-old had had his legs splayed and held, the cut made against screaming protests. Immediately afterwards, waves of his family had fallen upon him. They would grab his howling head and kiss it, then leave money on his bed. Oddly enough the money acted as a temporary anodyne, and the child's eyes would be distracted for anywhere between one and two seconds, before the pain returned. His father stood by beaming with pride; the mother waited outside, attempting smiles.

A party had begun in a long concreted hall, down the hill from Lado's house. The tables were piled with pyramids of plates, each course simply balanced on its predecessor. Every four seats there stood a collection of bottles: wine, vodka, *chacha*. As soon as the toasting began, the strangers were called to the head of the room, where an exhausted Taran told a predominantly Azerbaijani audience how much he admired the Georgian culture.

The evening progressed in a predictable manner. Many of the young men sought us out, speaking of their dreams to travel to America. Ilya did his best to dissuade them: 'In America, you have no mother, no father. Say you coming in, and you fall down on street, they no help you. They no give shit about you. America is angry place, they hate those that come. First, they hate Italians, then Jew, then Irish, now you. Stay home, you want to make money, make it here. I teach you. I show you American way of making money.'

Meanwhile, we clinked glasses and raised toast after toast to everybody's dreams. Dancing started, in time to a frantic beat. Women spun around men and I found myself led on to the dance floor, twirling in the arms of a fifty-year-old woman with a mouthful of gold teeth. Every time that she smiled, the light bulbs on the ceiling illuminated her mouth. Lado stepped up to the microphone. Our host, we now discovered, doubled as a wedding singer.

Everybody clapped, while whirling and drinking. Occasionally men paused to pat their foreheads with little white handkerchiefs, then they threw their hands in the air and stepped back on to the dance floor. Suddenly, a pair of firecrackers exploded in the room. The music faltered, then stopped.

'What was that?' shouted Taran above the thunder of noise.

'Firecrackers,' I screamed.

'It sounded like a pistol,' yelled John.

'Was gun,' shouted Ilya, grinning. 'This Caucasus.'

A crowd of people surrounded the offender, who was given away by the two large holes in the ceiling above his head and a shirt covered in plaster. The gunman was removed. He disappeared in a sea of drunken young men, who jolted, kicked and punched him through the room. The party was over, the shots considered an affront to the host. We stumbled up the hill to Lado's, where the party continued. John and I were asked to provide the entertainment, and boxing gloves were brought out from inside. Our bout was considered hysterical. We have, over the last couple of weeks, learned just enough to hurt each other, without the faintest idea of how to protect ourselves. When we were both dripping blood, the fight was called off. The experts gathered actually cried with laughter at the two friends determined to beat one another.

Taran elected to try his luck with the gloves again, but, to his surprise, Baklul volunteered to oppose him. It was almost as short a fight as Taran's first bout. Baklul, well versed from his prison days, immediately dropped under Taran's long arms and delivered a single, shuddering blow to our director's testicles. He returned to the concrete and the foolish foreigners were laughed at again. Ilya was holding his ribs, his eyes weeping tears of laughter.

A day later, we are travelling in the car, north of Tbilisi towards the Alazan River, which separates the plains of Georgia from the foothills of the Caucasus Mountains. Ahead lies the estate of Tsinondali, ancestral home of one of Georgia's oldest families, the Chavchavadzes. It rises from the lushest ground in the Caucasus. Either side of the road is heavy with undergrowth. Every few minutes, an ordered row of vineyards can be spotted. It is rich earth.

The house at Tsinondali, a large sprawling manor, painted bright white, is set amid brilliant green grass and a cloudless sky. It is surrounded by immaculate and blossoming gardens and in every way resembles an Edenic dream of rural life. We step out of the car and follow the eyes of our host, Merab Kokoshashvili, and his wife. He is a short man, well dressed with a trimmed silver beard and gentlemanly deportment. His grandparents were the last of the Chavchavadzes to live on their estate. All of Merab's grace is conveyed in the simple nod of a head: polite deference, under-standing, kindness, patience. It is not so hard to imagine him strolling through his grounds 150 years ago, greeting carriages of guests.

'This is not the same house,' he says, standing in front of his family's manor, now run by the state. 'It was of course burned down that day. Come, we will walk. You may read all you want of Shamil, but almost everything we know about him was from the months that followed. This is where you must spend time.'

The summer sun has not changed, nor the roll of the hills thirty miles to the north, nor even the design of the garden. It is an illu-sion of serenity that is perhaps only comprehensible early in the day, when the foothills to the east are still untouched by sun, like shadows waiting to be cast. All that is left from that day in 1854 is kept in a small glass cabinet on the ground floor of the house. A pair of silver candlesticks, engraved with the Chavchavadze mono-gram; a family Bible with a miniature portrait of its owner attached to its beaten front. Merab looks about him but does not speak. The earth beneath must still be marked with flecks of cinders and shards of wood from 4 July 1854.

'What do you think of the men who came that day?'

'I can understand,' he says slowly. 'I can understand why Shamil did it. I cannot justify it, but I understand it perfectly. This happened to my kin, to my family. It is in my blood and I feel it acutely.' He looks up and smiles. 'I am forever ambivalent.'

Merab shows us his family tree. It is a complicated matter, lines drawn between the dead reeling us back through the centuries, all the way to the birth of Georgia itself. Two sisters, Anna and Varvara, were born in the 1830s, granddaughters of George XIII, Georgia's last king, who had bequeathed his nation to the Tsar in 1801. The royal line claimed descent from King David. It is rumoured that until the rise of the Soviet Union, one of the old princesses insisted on wearing mourning on the Feast of the Assumption, believing that it was, after all, a bereavement in the family. Of the two sisters, the older, Anna, had married into the Chavchavadze family, one of the most distinguished in the country. The younger princess, Varvara, had suffered through a tragic last six months. Her husband, Ellico Orbeliani, had been killed fighting in Turkey. He left her with a six-month-old son, George, and a little girl who had succumbed to a fever just weeks after her father's death.

'It was a time', said Merab, 'when it was imperative to decide how Georgia would be developing. We were a province of Russia by then, had been for fifty years, yet many Georgians were now educated abroad, in England, in France, in Germany. Alexander Chavchavadze, Princess Anna's father-in-law, was the first man who arranged his estate in a European manner, the first to set his peasants free, to send them to cities to study. Dumas came here, Pushkin, Lermontov, Tolstoy, all outstanding thinkers.'

CHAPTER 16

# Hostages of Worth

*For Alexander Chavchavadze, the estate of Tsinondali may have been an oasis of concepts, where nations and peoples were redesigned for improvement, but for his extended family, in the summer of 1854, it was simply a place of quiet retreat, where serenity might be sought long enough to begin the process of recovery. Princess Orbeliani carried her six-month-old son with her and travelled with her niece, an eighteen-year-old beauty, Princess Nina Baratov.*

Accompanying the princesses was a French governess, Madame Drancy, who left behind a first-hand account of her days in the Caucasus. She found her first two weeks in Tsinondali delightful. 'The Princess showed me her magnificent garden. We admired the covered trellises of grapes, flower beds of jasmine, hundreds of different fruit trees.' Madame Drancy, in those initial days, was in constant awe of the richness of the soil and the myriad blooms that pushed their way upwards, as if their only duty was to delight the senses.

Anna Chavchavadze's husband, Prince David, was an aide-de-camp in Tbilisi as well as the head of the local militia at Tsinondali.

In peacetime, it was an idyllic life, allowing him to divide his days between his estate, his family and the affairs of the Alazan Valley. Often, he would arrive in time for dinner, delighting Madame Drancy with his European manners and always kneeling to greet his children. His portrait suggests an intelligent bemusement.

The day that David left, a torrential rain fell. He had been called two days' journey from Tsinondali, where it seemed that a force of fifteen thousand men was gathering to cross the Alazan. He believed it a feint by Shamil, for it was a deep river, hard to cross and had not been forded by the mountaineers in over fifty years. Now, with the heavens spilling summer rain into the mountains, the Alazan was so swollen that his slight worries receded further. This did not stop the women of Tsinondali from expressing concern, encouraged by their anxious peasants who had seen the constellation of Murid campfires lighting the horizon the night before.

In response to a letter written by his wife that let him know of the rumours of panic, he wrote, 'There is no occasion for uneasiness.' It would, then, have surprised him to discover that the messenger entrusted with the letter was butchered on the road. A day later, he received another letter from his nervous wife saying, 'Everyone is in a state of terror, all our neighbours have gone into the woods . . . your peasants have left. For God's sake, inform us whether we need take refuge anywhere.' He wrote again, 'There is no occasion for uneasiness.' This time he underlined the words. It would probably have been better for his household if the second messenger had suffered the same fate as the first.

Instead, though the mood was tense, the letter of comfort made up Princess Anna's mind. Ignoring the pleas of their fleeing peasants, the household staff, the children and the princesses remained in Tsinondali. Fires were seen again and the peasants were sure that these were so close that they must be on the Georgian side of the river. They tried to persuade the royals to retreat to the woods. Their doctor passed by, and reassured them that the latest news still placed the Lezgins, the neighbouring tribe to Shamil's Avars, on the other side of the banks. Finally, on a Saturday, with the fires still burning, the princesses decided that they must follow their neighbours into the woods and gathered their silver and diamonds, their best objects.

In the middle of such strained circumstances, when most sensible travellers were heading far from the Alazan River, a man arrived at their gates begging for permission to spend the night, claiming to be an Armenian merchant. He was soaked to the skin and claimed to have swum the Alazan River in an attempt to evade the mounting Lezgin forces. Princess Anna's state of mind can be guessed at. Madame Drancy always calls her the kindest of women, yet the governess heard her issue the order, 'Disarm him and if he tries to escape, shoot him.'

That night, all the women slept in the same room upstairs, the children curled on carpets, all the fires and lamps extinguished before the sun died, hoping to hide themselves in darkness and silence. Unfortunately, the moon was full and the whitewashed house must have stood out against the night like a burning star. At four in the morning, they heard a shot ring out. They looked at one another. No other shots followed. Madame Drancy could not return to sleep but crept about the garden, noting how calm everything was, how the ceaseless tone of the cicadas seemed to pause that night. Looking over an embankment, behind the house, she saw two Murid scouts picking a path over a small stream. She ran back to the bedroom where she related what she had seen. The princesses knew that it was too late to leave the estate, but hoped that by moving to the attic they might not be discovered by the marauders.

At eight in the morning, the first men arrived in the house, a small advance party whose intrusion must have increased the levels of fear of those hiding above. The women could not stop the children crying, nor the nursemaids from weeping in fear. Then came a thunderous approach of hooves, and, peeking from the attic window, Madame Drancy noted that the entire courtyard was filled with 'horses and turbans'. She continued to write, 'We heard their terrible cries, the sound of glass breaking, of furniture being demolished, of silverware falling from smashed cabinets.'

More peculiarly, it seemed that every Lezgin and Avar who entered Tsinondali could not resist slamming his hands down on one of the two pianos. The women sank to their knees and prayed to God that they would not be found. Half an hour passed in looting before they heard footsteps come to their door. Princess Orbeliani stood closest to the door. She had lost a child and husband in the last six months and refused to see another person die. If they were intent on murder, then at least she would be spared the anguish of seeing others suffer. There was more shouting, then the gathering of a small force and once, twice, three times the door held before breaking, sending a wave of raiders spilling into the room of terrified women. The raiders paused in shock, then, to the women's surprise, burst into laughter. Not knowing what lay behind the locked door, they had presumed that it was an armed force, not a gathering of defenceless women. Their laughter was muffled by the screams of the terrified children. Each woman and child was grabbed by a man who then turned, dragging his prisoner downstairs.

The staircase was a sea of confusion, men carrying children and women coming down, men holding silverware and swords rushing up. What none of them could know was that without Princess Anna Chavchavadze's permission the last of her husband's peasants, before fleeing to the woods, had taken it upon himself to start to saw down the staircase, believing he would then make it impossible for a raiding party to reach the attic. When Princess Anna had discovered him at work she had stopped him, fearing that the Murids would burn them out should they hear the children and not be able to reach them. Now, under such pressure, the weakened staircase snapped. Madame Drancy remembered a sharp crack and then falling the two floors, held in her captor's arms, her skirts grasped by a screaming lady's maid. They were stunned, but otherwise unharmed, pulled roughly upright and out to the courtyard. Madame Drancy looked about her for the princesses and her young charges but saw no one until she came into the bright sunlight. There, amid hundreds of circling horses, screaming men and upturned carts, Madame Drancy was stripped of her clothes, until she was wearing only her petticoat and boots. She saw her two students strapped to the flanks of a large horse. Princess Anna was lying prostrate on the ground, her foot badly gashed, her youngest child clasped to her. When Madame Drancy tried to move to her, she was cut across the shoulders by a whip. In the middle of the cries and confusion sat the youngest princess, eighteen-year-old Nina Baratov, who had been placed on a fine roan horse, apparently untouched, still fully clothed and in possession of all her jewels. She was being led through the chaos by a young Chechen and no one sought to stop him.

Once all the captives were secured, the house was pillaged by two hundred pairs of hands at once. It took little time, the spoils brought to the courtyard and fought over, the most prized possessions, after silver, being sugar and tea. Once all the local cattle and buffalo had been herded towards the main house, the decision was made to leave. The absurd train of Chechens, Lezgins and Avars, draped in French cloths, wearing children's hats, riding with captives on the backs of their horses amid a trail of bellowing cows, arced out of Tsinondali and headed towards the foothills.

Madame Drancy, having become soaked crossing a small river, let her mind drift towards the future. Her captor wrapped her in his native *bourka*. She had decided that she would remain captive no more than three years, so that her son back in Paris would only be eleven by the time of her return. She believed that in that time she could teach a sympathetic mountaineer the French language and persuade him to assist her in escape. The governess did not know who had been taken, who had escaped, who had died. That night she finally came across Princess Anna, still clutching her small child, Lydia. She, like Madame Drancy, had been stripped of all her clothes, her lower leg still bloody from the cut received during her fall from the stairs. She told the Frenchwoman that they tried to take her daughter from her, but with the bribe of a pair of pearl earrings, sympathy had been extended and her daughter returned.

It was only now, during the first of many days' travel, that Madame Drancy realized the full extent of the expedition. They were far from the only captives. Most, instead of being slung or carried on horses, had been made to walk and beaten every time they paused for breath. They arrived late at the muddled camp, and, according to the governess, there were well over a hundred prisoners taken from the Georgian lowlands. The Murids stopped by a river and prayed, making their ablutions and thanking Allah for the success of their raid.

The members of the column continued towards the Alazan River, driving their horses into the swollen torrents and swimming across. Nina Baratov, her arms tied to her side, fell from her horse during the crossing and was dragged out of the water by her dress. Madame Drancy was again soaked to the skin, and, more alarmingly, was the subject of bickering between tribesmen. One resentful servant, perhaps with a grudge against the Frenchwoman, had informed a tribesman that the governess worked wonderfully with needle and thread. He tried to buy her off her current captor, but Princess Orbeliani happened to ride by in time to invent the explanation that Madame Drancy was the wife of a famous French general and would be worth much in ransom. Madame Drancy reports the episode with a touch of pride. She recounts that she was valued at the equivalent of twelve francs, while she had witnessed them arguing over a Georgian woman for the sum of fifty centimes.

Had anyone else defended Madame Drancy, it would perhaps have ended badly, but the raiders all knew the Orbeliani name. The princess's husband had been a prisoner of Shamil for over six months and had, during the time, earned a reputation for bravery, the highest ideal of the mountain men. All knew of him, and now the princess was constantly assailed by riders who had heard of her presence and galloped up to look at the gallant man's wife and to see his young son. One Chechen even stopped beating a nurse long enough to find some sugar for the child.

All about them were these pendulum swings of kindness and cruelty, most of the kindness directed at the valuable hostages and most of the cruelties at the captured peasants. Passing through a narrow defile, Madame Drancy's musings were interrupted by a volley of gunfire. The prisoners could not know it, but a company had been sent ahead to try to prevent the raiding party from reaching the mountains. Some of the first Chechens were shot from their saddles, the rest wheeled, grabbed their hostages close and galloped in the opposite direction. The ambush was poorly timed, the first shot fired too early.

Clutching her daughter Lydia to her side, Princess Anna held tight to her captor, who yelled in excitement and whipped his horse to greater speeds. Princess Anna's hands were still numb from the frozen mountain waters of the Alazan and she knew she would not be able to hold her daughter for long. She screamed at her captor to stop, at least long enough for her to secure the child. Instead he galloped onwards and Lydia continued to slip from the princess's grasp. She only had the child's leg now, the baby screaming with pain as the motion of the horse beat her back and forth. Princess Anna let her child slip, but her captor, in the van of the charging raiders, did not rein in his mount. Instead, the child lay in the path of a thousand horses. No man would stop.

They drew breath only when they reached the captured Russian outpost of Pohali. There, Princess Anna wandered through the captives, hoping that someone had picked up her fallen child. Though some knew the baby's fate, no one dared speak. Pohali had acted as Shamil's command post during the last week and now his entire army was gathered, almost fifteen thousand men. Somehow, in this dense mass, Princess Anna came across her captured cousin Ivan Chavchavadze. He was horrified with the sight of the badly bruised matriarch, shoulders clotted with blood and no skin left on her feet. Princess Anna had been the best treated of all the prisoners.

The horror of the previous day dawned most slowly on David Chavchavadze. He had had good reason to send his comforting letters to Tsinondali. His spies had informed him that the major push across the Alazan would be directed towards the town of Shildi. With only five hundred men at his disposal, he deployed his troops in ambush along the only road. On 1 and 2 July, they had lain in wait and on the 3rd, confirming the intelligence, Shildi was attacked by a large Murid horde. It had then been, in full confidence, that Chavchavadze had informed his wife that there was no reason to panic. He was very busy repulsing a feint, inducing a large number of casualties on the enemy, but he could not know just how strong their main force had been.

When a second report detailed an alternate charge of horse-men into the unguarded flat lands, Chavchavadze was dubious. He sought high ground and there, thirty miles before him, lay a series of villages in flames. Soldiers, for better of for worse, believe in duty. Chavchavadze, the father, wanted to direct his entire company to his own estate to rescue his family. Instead, he answered a desperate call of help from the failing garrison at Shildi.

He could not be certain, but he believed he could see Tsinondali in flames. He sent a section of the native militia to the ravaged neighbourhood. They returned at nightfall with a detailed report. They had come across small bands of Chechens who had continued to loot the area, and brought their heads as evidence. They had found five raiders in a church and burned them out. As was their custom, they presented not only the Chechen heads to David Chavchavadze but also any spoils they had recovered. A sack was emptied in front of him. He recognized a pair of candlesticks, objects from his nursery. Chavchavadze was incredulous.

A breathless messenger rode in, with the report that a hostage train had been engaged across the river. A handful of mountaineers and prisoners had been killed outright, while a few captives had been recovered. So great was Chavchavadze's shock that he clung to the belief that his family was hiding in the woods, and sent a small detachment to the scene of the unsuccessful ambush to search for the wounded.

Only on 6 July did Chavchavadze allow himself the time to return home. His hopes were dashed. He had guessed that his estate had been reduced to ashes, but he had not expected to find his land littered with the charred bodies of his peasants. Tied to a tree, delirious from her ordeal, was the family's oldest nurse, whom the Chechens had not thought worth taking. She had raised David Chavchavadze, and his father before him. For those long days, she had had no option but to face the remains of the house that had been her home for seventy years.

There was no sign of the rest of his family. It was only then that one of his men confessed his knowledge. The body of Lydia had been found across the river. To spare the prince's grief, he had buried her alone, in the neighbouring church of St George, one of the few buildings in the immediate area that had been spared firing.

# CHAPTER 17

# Walking over the Past

*Merab rises from the long grasses of his garden and smiles at the distant sound of children playing, screams of delight rising over a maze of rosebushes. Some places seem to retain echoes of the past better than others, haunted by sadness, but Tsinondali seems bright and alive. Perhaps it is because the new house rests on top of the old; every structure on the property has been levelled and rebuilt since its destruction. As a place, Tsinondali wasn't maimed, it was annihilated, which has allowed a rebirth rather than sorrowful echoes of burned timbers and shattered buildings.*

Only in the woods behind the house, thick enough to be dark in daylight, can you summon a sense of that July day. In the middle of a small clearing stands an old oak tree, subject of local myths. Its hollow centre is big enough to hold one body, yet a guide announces that three peasants hid here for two days. When questioned the story is changed. She now says that little Lydia passed the night there in safety, this despite the fact that she was barely old enough to crawl, and was by the evening lying dead over twenty miles away.

Merab steers us past enormous wooden barrels into the vast banqueting hall that stands as the centrepiece of the estate's continued wine production. Inside stretches an ancient oaken table. Above are a pair of windows that send angled shafts of light pouring over the chairs. The room seems to reinforce the fragility that lies at the heart of Tsinondali. The cultivated land, sculpted gardens and encouragement of free thought will always be vulnerable to any fires that might blow south from the mountains.

We sit back in our chairs. Ilya is billowing the smoke from his cigarette into the dusty pillars of light, a glassful of wine in his right hand. He tilts his head back and empties it in one long gulp. His mind is always ticking, finding ways to ameliorate or antagonize within moments. Ilya is a great connoisseur of the ephemeral: money must be spent, food eaten, cups drained. Everything is a reaction and perhaps this is why he enjoys causing and watching the reactions of others. Right now he is blissfully and deliberately ignoring Taran's requests for help in filming. Work is not high on his list of priorities, leastways when it interrupts enjoyment. He has finally worn down Taran. Help from Ilya is not something the director has come to rely on. If Ilya cannot be roused in the morning, Taran puts his equipment on his own back and marches out for his day's work. John tends to shake his head and mutter, 'God damned Uzbek.' Ilya always cackles and repeats the latest insult cast in his direction. It is a wonderfully frustrating strategy that no one has learned to outwit.

With Merab beside us, we leave the estate and drive towards the Alazan River to reach the village of Gremi, following in the path of the retreating marauders. Until the seventeenth century Gremi was the capital of the region, but was razed by the Persian

Shah Abbas in 1614. Those who were not killed were driven from the city. The ruins stand looking towards the mountains – brittle, accusing shells. All that remains is a fortified church that sits on an outcrop of rock, a stone pulpit surveying the lowlands. Tonight the landscape has been soaked in redness by the dying sun, all the greens turned black, but the orange sands are lit like a bed of coals.

'In war,' said Merab, as we climb towards the belfry-tower, 'there is no time for peaceful labour. The Chechens were never farmers, yet they needed the means to eat and drink, to feed themselves. It was a difficult time for them. They came here, pillaged one of the richest estates in Georgia, and took the family. This was, I suppose, their idea of an economy.'

Merab pauses and points along the road. 'In 1880,' he continues, 'the locals caught a Chechen close to Tsinondali with a hostage. He was hung from a tree by his hands. Two knife slits were cut down each of his sides, then they rubbed two pounds of salt into his wounds. They walked away and left him to die. But now, once again, they are kidnapping. Russian generals, wealthy men. They get ransoms, it is how they subsist. Nobody can work in Chechnya now. The old refineries are either closed down or destroyed, the pipeline is always sabotaged. It is kidnapping again, the same business as one hundred and fifty years ago. This is the logic of things.'

Merab's finger traces the path through the foothills that the train of stolen goods and hostages followed. 'Be patient with Tsinondali,' he advises. 'Try to understand that of all the wars of those forty years, it was there in the months of hostage taking, in what happened between Shamil and my family, that there is much to understand.' It is good advice. Almost everything that can be learned from firsthand accounts of the Imam comes from the year following the strike on Tsinondali. To concentrate on it may seem disproportionate, but it is by far the most revealing period of the Murid Wars.

The mountains ahead are composed of three layers, each one dwarfing the one in front, like a series of rising waves. They look too steep to accept people, let alone horses. To the genteel women who had climbed them in 1854, they must have seemed tortuous and forbidding.

# CHAPTER 18

# Guests of the Mountains

*Little George's nurse was murdered during the first week's climb;*
*she had not been able to keep up with the horses. The Lezgins,*
*viewing her as the sole reason they were slowed, slit her throat*
*and left her body by the rough track. She had been hampered*
*by wounds suffered in the initial attack on Tsinondali. Madame*
*Drancy reports that 'her head was covered in blood. Her left*
*hand was mutilated; the index fingers almost completely*
*detached.' A Georgian child, unable to stop himself from crying,*
*was picked up by the feet and brained against the side of a rock*
*in front of Princess Nina Baratov.*

Often during their steep journey, rains fell, leaving the exhausted
hostages shivering with cold. When Madame Drancy stumbled across
a familiar face, they would barely have the energy to speak, but would
simply hold each other and cry. Strangely, she had time to appreciate the beauty about her, commenting on fallen trees covered in soft
moss, on little red birds that hopped from branch to branch and the
green lizards that ran in front of them. She noticed rhododendrons,

and azaleas with red flowers that her Lezgin captors liked to cut and eat. She also never forgot the tracks of ice, still covering the mountainside in early July, when she was forced to hold on to the tail of a horse and was dragged, stumbling and slipping, ever upwards.

Twice their journey was broken by short stays in *aouls*. The first acts of true kindness shown to the prisoners came through the actions of an old mullah in the larger *aoul*. He killed a sheep for the captives, was gentleman enough not to enter the small room where the women were held prisoner and gave money to a young captive to buy a chicken from a local. The mullah even managed to persuade a neighbouring family to lend the captives a pot to cook their chicken in, a considerable feat, since dishes used by infidels would have to be washed not once, but seven times.

Five full weeks after their capture in Tsinondali, the captives reached the *aoul* of Dargo, Shamil's well-defended capital. Madame Drancy describes it as standing beneath a landscape of eternal snows. They arrived in the middle of a downpour, the captives cowering under *bourkas*, as thunder rolled through the mountains. The *aoul* was surrounded by a moat and a thick palisade of branches, holding a permanent population of four hundred natives, swelled by Shamil's immediate troop of two hundred Murids whenever the Imam was present.

The women were escorted through the narrow alleys of the *aoul*, then through three doors until they found themselves in Shamil's seraglio. They removed their boots and were shown into a small white room, little better than a cell, with a ceiling not more than six feet high. The only window was the size of a pocket handkerchief, the only furniture a bench and a threadbare carpet. A pile of clothes had been left for them to choose from. A dish of mutton, rice and raisins was brought into the room, along with water, honey and bread. And then, one by one, Shamil's wives entered. The first,

Zaidette, was the coldest and most temperamental. In the months ahead, the relationship between Zaidette and her prisoners was to sway wildly, from moments of great understanding to threats of death. Madame Drancy was convinced that, since Zaidette was mistress of the seraglio's provisions, the amount of attention Shamil paid to the oldest of his wives was in direct correlation to the quality of food she granted the prisoners. Brewing jealousy or an argument with her husband would result in stale bread dipped in grease. Occasionally, she would forget to feed them altogether.

It was obvious to all the prisoners that Shuanette was the Imam's favourite. At thirty-two, the princesses agreed that she remained the prettiest and kindest of them all. Only Madame Drancy could find a hole to pick, claiming that her large hands and feet betrayed her vulgar origins. She was an Armenian, captured in a raid similar to that on Tsinondali, in the village of Mozdock. Her entire family had been brought to Dargo, but her mother, father, sisters and brothers had been released once she had agreed to marry the Imam. Her father had no wish to leave his daughter behind and offered Shamil vast sums of money to set her free. What he could not account for was that Anna, as she was called before her conversion to Islam, was receptive to Shamil's advances. She volunteered to stay and within two years had learned to read the Koran. Despite her love for the Imam, she often confessed to the princesses that her heart ached for her family. The occasional concerned visits of her brothers to Dargo constantly pulled her between the twin ideals of freedom and love.

The youngest of Shamil's wives was called Amina, a beautiful woman who had married the Imam four years before at the age of fourteen. Madame Drancy noted her perfect oval face, and moreover an unequalled generosity of character. The princesses remembered her wrapping lambskin shoes about the feet of two prisoners to protect them from a march in the snow. Still, Madame Drancy manages to have the last word, deciding that 'her mouth was too big, though she had perfect teeth'.

On their second day in Dargo, they were warned that Shamil would visit. He did not enter the room, but sat outside on a simple wooden stool. At sixty-five, wearing white robes that focused the eye on his long red beard, Shamil is compared by Madame Drancy to a lion in repose. 'His expression', she said, 'was calm, imposing, but generally soft.' When looking at his prisoners, he preferred to keep his grey eyes half closed, as if they were in danger of leaking his secrets. Even Madame Drancy can find little fault, concluding that he was, in every way, 'a superior man'. She found his sobriety remarkable, noting that he ate only bread, rice, honey and fruit. He drank nothing but tea and water, and was, noted the Frenchwoman, 'in extraordinary health'.

This portrait seems incredible: the myths spun in the valleys of northern Georgia and southern Russia had painted him as a monster. Both he and Hadji Murad had even been accused of eating Russian flesh. Yet, in 1854 we are informed, through Georgian and Russian accounts, that this was a man who loved all children, who divided his time equally between his wives and silent communion with Allah. His absences over the next eight months not only affected the moods of his wives, but even came to sadden his captives.

Shamil told the gathered women how he usually employed prisoners building or repairing roads, but they had been captured for a specific reason. For years, he had sought prisoners of importance. Indeed, he had presumed that Prince Orbeliani, his captive for over six months, might have been weighty enough for his purposes. All that he wished for, he confessed, was the return of his son, captured fourteen years before by the Russians. The princesses would not be released, he informed them, unless Jamal al-Din was sent to him from St Petersburg.

Shamil's first request of his captives was that they were to sit and write letters, begging for their release and stating the Imam's demand for the return of his son. He gave them letters that had already been written to the captives, but was puzzled by one missive that was not in Russian, Georgian or Tatar. Though it was simply a letter addressed in French for Madame Drancy from her mother, Shamil believed it might be a coded message of trickery. He informed them that it was written within the laws of Allah that he might decapitate his hostages. The princesses would have known the truth of this. Twelve years before, at the end of lengthy negotiations for the release of ten officers, a message was smuggled to the captives baked within a loaf of bread. It said nothing of import, simply instructing them to prepare themselves for their journey to freedom. The message was discovered, duplicity presumed, and all ten officers were immediately beheaded.

The captives' initial terror at imprisonment was lessened by two factors. First, Shamil's character convinced them that he was a man of his word. Once he had spoken of their release, hope was allowed to grow. Second, they found his favourite wife, Shuanette, much to their liking. She showed them numerous small acts of kindness that were magnified by their vulnerable position, from obtaining carpets and blankets for the approaching winter to showering affection on the captive children.

The next seven months presented many problems. Both the young princes fell sick. Little Alexander was diagnosed by a Lezgin woman, who melted lead in water and held it against his head. When the lead formed the shape of a caterpillar it indicated, she said, that he had worms. George was treated to the same examination, but since the lead assumed the shape of a bird's beak, the woman announced that someone, driven by jealousy, had placed the evil eye on the child. It was only when Princess Anna

Chavchavadze also fell ill that Shamil allowed a man to be sent down into the valleys for medicine. Within weeks they had all recovered. Madame Drancy dedicated their cure to neither the Lezgin nor to medicine, but to their youth and strength of character. Any ill-health suffered in the next months terrified the governess. She knew full well that all children orphaned as captives were bound, according to the laws of Allah, to be raised as Muslims.

In November, bad news arrived. Messengers who were passing constantly between David Chavchavadze and Shamil brought word that although money had been raised for their release, there was no word from St Petersburg about the demand for the return of Jamal al-Din. It angered the Imam greatly and, sending for the princesses, he related how his *naibs* often approached him with offers to purchase his captives. Should his son not be returned, he said, he would distribute them to his favourite lieutenants, and they would be lost for ever to the mountains. In an understandable state of panic, they were asked to write once more to their families.

The greatest relief throughout their captivity, to both Madame Drancy and the princesses, was how well the children were treated even during the most tense of times. The armed guards at the gate of the seraglio would often lift them up into their arms, keeping their little hands away from the sharp edges of their *kindjals*. The children had no fear of the Imam and if they spotted him crossing the courtyard towards his rooms, they would run to him, and were always rewarded with either a piece of fruit or a coin that could buy enough eggs or a chicken to give them relief from the diet of bread and cheeses. Dressed in little more than rags, with their heads shaved in the summer custom, it must have been hard to distinguish the little princes from the Imam's own children.

Distractions during these seven months were few, the most memorable when Amina smuggled the princesses into her rooms, from where they could watch the men of the *aoul* competing in feats of horsemanship. The rider would bring his horse to a gallop then pick up small objects from the ground. Whenever he was at Dargo, these tournaments were usually won by Ghazi Muhammed, Shamil's son and heir. On another occasion, they witnessed a wedding in Dargo, amazed that the newly-weds were kept in separate rooms, unable to see one another for three days, while the rest of the *aoul* celebrated.

In Madame Drancy's account, it seems as if a strange symbiotic relationship formed between the princesses and Shamil's wives, most particularly Amina and Shuanette, both of whom had been born outside the mountains. While the Georgian ladies depended on Shamil's wives for their charity, it was clear to the Frenchwoman that the wives were little better than prisoners themselves. Together, they formed a bastion against boredom, where information and stories were swapped, keeping at bay the dullness of their days. On every occasion Madame Drancy felt overwhelmed by despair, she simply looked at her fellow captives and found herself 'happy to suffer with the noble souls of the princesses'. Still, tears poured down and prayers were sent upwards every day. This never failed to shock the Imam's wives, who were, for the most part, happy to have 'guests'. The three wives even began to attend Madame Drancy's French lessons for the young princes, finding endless fascination in the strange words.

Despite the efforts of friendship on both sides, the underlying tensions and differences made true understanding an impossibility. A particular friendship had been struck up between Shamil's youngest wife, Amina, and Nina Baratov. They shared a similar age and beauty. Together they used to tease Khadji, Shamil's chief steward, the most devout of Muslims. To Amina's delight, the young princess would accidentally brush past him, and though he would hold his tongue, the touch of the unclean was forever condemning him to the irritating ritual of washing seven times. One night, Amina joined Nina in the princesses' room and together they watched from the door as the Imam crossed the courtyard to visit his youngest wife. Dressed in his white shoubu that trailed like a train upon the floor, Shamil waited patiently by Amina's door, never hearing the giggles of the young women. Finally, exasperated, he gave up and returned to his quarters.

Talking one day of her hopes for release, Nina was interrupted by Amina, who praised her character and told her that Jamal al-Din would, if he returned from Russia, take her as his wife. Nina Baratov did not filter her thoughts through politics or diplomacy, but reacted angrily. She berated Shamil for cursing them with a thousand tortures and said that she would, in the end, rather die than submit to such a hateful union. Only six months before, Nina had caused a dozen hearts to quicken their beats in the ballrooms of St Petersburg. She had found Tsinondali removed enough to make her aunts despair of her moodiness; Amina's suggestion that she might spend the rest of her days enclosed within the seraglio of a Muslim mountaineer unleashed a reaction of true horror.

Unfortunately, Amina related Nina's reaction to Zaidette, Shamil's oldest wife. Princess Orbeliani, as Nina's aunt and guardian, did her best to appease the gathering of angry women. They entered the room, and in front of Madame Drancy began to berate the young princess. 'Do you know that after Mohammed, Shamil is the first servant of Allah on earth? Do you know that you are all his prisoners and that he has the right to sell you? You do not deserve the honour of marrying his son.' Even Shuanette, forever their supporter, chastised the young girl, for, to her, Shamil was beyond reproach. The princess explained that for her niece it was a matter of faith, and that her reaction was only due to the hurtful thought of converting from Christianity. This did not prevent Zaidette from approaching the Imam, but thankfully Shamil considered it a matter of bickering women. His concerns were greater. His son Ghazi Muhammed had been wounded, though not badly, and the Imam felt the tide of battle was against him.

Some days later, the Imam announced that in addition to Jamal al-Din, he would also be demanding one million roubles for his prisoners' release. It was a preposterous sum. Shamil knew that the princesses were ladies in waiting to the Tsarina, and was encouraged by his *naibs* in the belief that he was free to demand all the money in Russia. A St Petersburg journal had made its way up the mountains, and there the Imam's translators had found mention of a large sum of money, a million-pound loan granted by the British Government. His *naibs* believed that this should be a similar transaction: every *aoul* destroyed by the Russians would now be rebuilt with Georgian money. In three days, Shamil added, if his wishes were not met, the women would be dispersed among his *naibs*. The princesses did not weep like Madame Drancy, but simply prayed.

There is a story, perhaps apocryphal, that Princess Anna's descendant Merab told in Tsinondali. Anna believed that neither Shamil nor his *naibs* had any idea what kind of sum a million was. Talking to Shamil about the impossibility of ever raising such an amount, she begged him that he would only have to look at one million of anything to know how outrageous the demand was. That night, Shamil's mullah began to count with beans. When he was still counting, a day and a half later, Shamil admitted that the figure was larger than he had thought.

Part of the reason why the princesses had suffered through eight months as hostages was that Jamal al-Din was not in St Petersburg, but had been stationed in Warsaw with the Vladimirski Lancers. He had been completely Russified over the course of the last fourteen years. As a favourite of the Tsar, he did not question Russia's right to territorial conquest, and never even thought of Poland as an occupied country. The majority of his regiment had been sent to fight in the Crimea. He was not only disappointed in being left behind, but had volunteered to fight the tribes of the Caucasus.

With Russia now at war against France, Britain, Turkey and the Caucasian tribes, the Tsar felt himself surrounded and harried. When a message reached Jamal al-Din that Nicholas wished to see him in St Petersburg, he did not hesitate and sped to Nicholas's side. With such a blind belief in duty, Jamal al-Din was always likely to submit to his fate. The news of the raid on Tsinondali shocked him. As the Tsar's ward in St Petersburg, he would have most certainly met, perhaps even have danced with, the Tsarina's ladies in waiting. There is no doubt that his return to the mountains was a courageous act of selflessness and duty, rather than a desire to become once more the son of Shamil.

Jamal al-Din had grown up to be a slim, handsome figure, popular in the courts of St Petersburg, not only because he was the finest horseman in the Academy, but also because the Tsar had treated him as a godson since his arrival. In a photograph dated 1854, taken in St Petersburg, the young man looks out, wide eyed. It is unlikely that he would have sat for such a portrait before seeing the Tsar. It is, then, the face of a man who already knows his fate: he has a puzzled look about him, a delicate hesitancy that borders on confusion.

In Vladikavkaz, at the steps of the Caucasus, Jamal al-Din and his small escort of Cossacks were greeted by David Chavchavadze. The young man's stoicism was appreciated by all the officers. While he had not been born a Russian, they all knew the extent of the sacrifice that he was making. Chavchavadze wrote that Jamal al-Din only mentioned his return once, saying, 'At the very hour when I begin to appreciate the advantages of learning and am ready with all my heart and soul to apply myself, fate flings me back into the midst of ignorance, where I shall probably forget all I learned, and go backwards, like a crab.' Chavchavadze also made a sad note of Jamal al-Din's luggage: it consisted almost entirely of books, papers and inks.

Once he was within sight of the Caucasus, he must also have known that eyes were looking down upon him. Lowland spies reported his behaviour to the *aouls*. They learned that he spoke only Russian, danced mazurkas, wore the uniform of a military officer. Messengers came and went between the two camps, carrying Shamil's threats of distributing the princesses to the *naibs* and a continued dull demand for the impossible million roubles. This was no longer Shamil's doing, but his *naibs* were insistent that such a sum was possible.

A formal meeting was arranged between David Chavchavadze and Jamal al-Din and Shamil's ambassadors. It was hoped that the final details might be worked out. However, Chavchavadze was presented with a new letter from Shamil. It expressed thanks for the imminent return of his son, but now insisted once more on the million roubles and added the condition of the release of 150 captured Murids. The negotiations had always been tense, but with Jamal al-Din and the princesses less than a hundred miles from one another, Chavchavadze could no longer stomach these oscillations of demand. He had raised forty thousand roubles, an immense sum in itself, necessitating the sale of all his property, including the estate of Tsinondali.

A furious Chavchavadze told one of Shamil's ambassadors:

If by Saturday you do not bring the solemn acceptance of my offer, you may do what you like with my family. They will no longer be mine. Tell your Imam that I have always been grateful to him for the manner in which he has respected my family, but if he carries out the threat of sending them to the *aouls*, I renounce them. I will leave here and take Jamal al-Din with me. And if, after I have fulfilled my threat, Shamil could offer to give me back my family for nothing, together with all the treasures he possesses, I swear by God that I will not receive them back.[12]

Shamil's ambassadors begged for a week to return with an answer, then added that it might be possible for him to have his wife back in return for Jamal al-Din and the forty thousand roubles they had been offered, but Princess Orbeliani and her family would remain in Dargo. At this point, with Chavchavadze stunned by such duplicity, the Murid interpreter turned to Jamal al-Din and whispered, 'Do not be upset . . . all will end well.'

'I am not upset,' roared Jamal al-Din. 'I am no longer an Avar. I would go back to Russia tomorrow if I could.' This, in turn, disturbed Shamil's ambassadors, so that the tent, instead of being filled by the calming prospect of peace, was now bristling with affront. No agreements were reached and the ambassadors were hurriedly escorted from the camp.

It was Georgian against Chechen, Avar against Russian, and not just within the tent, but within the men themselves. It was decided that a more delicate hand would be needed to conduct such explosive negotiations. The only potential candidate for such a challenge was an officer who had always dealt well with dualities. Isaac Gramov was, by birth, Armenian. As well as his native language, he was fluent in Russian and Georgian. His childhood had been spent in the foothills of the Caucasus and he had added to his linguistic arsenal a smattering of the dialects of the mountain tribes.

# CHAPTER 19

# The Highwire of History

*There are now only four of us. Mr Ramiz has returned to Baku.*

*Ilya and Mr Ramiz were half a bottle of vodka away from homicide and one had to leave. Though Ilya was the more provocative of the two, a return to Azerbaijan was a simpler option than a flight to America. On the morning that Ramiz left the two were even showing a willingness to negotiate through past offences. They shared a small, insincere hug and then off drove Mr Ramiz in his Jeep that we had called home these past six weeks.*

Our host, Lado, now sleeps on the concrete porch on a cot, ejected from the marital bed for an unknown crime. Discord has seeped through the entire community. We had woken Lado early this morning. A brief discussion ensued, his brother Baklul appeared. We would rent one of their identical taxis for a ten- or twelve-day journey into Armenia. It didn't matter which taxi, they were both small, orange Ladas, the Russian equivalent of a Ford Cortina. Both cars were built in the 1970s, both employed a canny use of string for seat-belts and both had splintered back and front windscreens. We agreed that should the taxi be stolen we would owe our hosts no more than two hundred American dollars. Lado's last gesture, before settling back into his cot, was to give us directions to the Armenian border.

Six hours later we have rumbled through a dirt road, pausing every few miles to fill water bottles in the river that parallels our course. Ilya sprays the water over the engine and we wait patiently under the broiling sun as the car cools off. Rusted Jeeps roll past, donating brief, encouraging waves. Finally, we hit a stretch of tarmac.

'Where are we?' we ask a man selling watermelons by the side of the road.

'Twenty minutes from Tbilisi,' comes the answer. Lado had recommended the longest short-cut in Georgia. We had gone up and over a mountain on a dirt track, instead of circumventing it on one of Georgia's few perfectly paved roads.

Our one contact in Armenia is a man called Ararat Sargsyan. In his forties, he brings us back to a house he built with his own hands, where his wife, their twin daughters and son await. It proves to be a strange week, our journey in Armenia directed by Ararat's kindness. Never has a man taken the duties of a host to such an extreme. Meal after meal is provided, his son Arshak becomes our guide, his friends open their houses to us, encourage us to visit. The warmth is all-encompassing, having the odd effect of making me feel a touch of homesickness. We are no longer on the road, but living within a family structure.

Ararat, portly and dignified, can smile with undiluted sincerity, a feat that can relax a roomful of strangers. His friends consist of a colony of artists: the writer Samvel, who learned his English from smuggled Beatles records; the sculptor Saak, whose work of a giant penis riding a horse leaves Ilya agog; Nadia, a ballerina with dark sleepy eyes. Arshak, his own son, is an artist with a remarkable ability to conjure and caricature the life about him. He has already had his first exhibition, before his eighteenth birthday.

'It is very strange,' says Ararat, sitting in his kitchen, 'we have had three guests from far away this year. Every guest is a writer.' He points at my pen. 'They come, they sit, they write. My two girls, they think that if you are foreign this is what you do. Every man from far away is a writer.'

Ararat sips his tea. 'You live in America, yes?'

Taran and I nod. John shakes his head.

'Where you live, John?'

'Baku,' confesses the photographer, naming the capital city of Armenia's historical enemy.

'Ahhh,' says Ararat, 'you come into my house as a spy, but you will leave as a double agent.'

Ararat also works with words, having just finished a series of printed alphabets from the ancient world. The globular script of the Hittites, the prison-like scratches of the Celts, the ethereal swirls of Easter Island and, of course, the thirty-six letters of the Armenian alphabet appear in his series. His works seem mystical, dense signs that challenge understanding and yet promote it, a perfect introduction to any concept of Armenia. Armenian pride starts with her words, all drawn from the oldest alphabet in the world, entirely phonetic. The lavash bread that signals the start of every meal is as thin as paper; it looks like parchment, a scroll that might be inked in Armenian letters, then used to pass knowledge through the generations.

Armenia is a country well aware of its history. The Russian travel writer Bitov noted, in his journey to Yerevan in 1960, that there was no house he entered which did not have the familiar three volumes of Leo's *History of Armenia*. It is, then, strange to us that in a week of talking to artists, writers, philosophers and politicians, no one can remember the name of Imam Shamil.

Armenia's geographical position, almost as much as her history, lies at the heart of the explanation. Like the northern Caucasus, the Transcaucasus has long been buffered by the prevailing winds of history. But the memory is tempered by loss. One of the greatest empires was Armenian, stretching between the seas, and the more you talk, the more you realize that though the empire was lost in AD 120, for many this remains recent history. As Alexandre Dumas said during his travels in the Caucasus in 1858, 'for [an Armenian] Abraham died yesterday and Jacob is still alive'.

Armenia is often thought of as an international victim, a country betrayed most notably in the shuffling loyalties of the First World War. As with the case of the Holocaust, the crimes committed against the Armenians were so repellent, the numbers so overwhelming, that they left a deep and unsettling scar on the national conscience. In the forced marches conducting Armenians from Turkish-occupied land, the chances of survival were minuscule. Out of the 18,000 exiles from Sebastia and Kharberd, there were 350 survivors, all women and children; of the 19,000 banished in Arzrum, there were 11 survivors.

A German eyewitness in 1917 reported Armenians bound by hands and feet and hung upside down in the streets, a scene from an abattoir. A man would go down the line with an axe, splitting skulls. Fathers were tied to chairs, their children dismembered before them. The German continued, 'They choke women to death by forcing into their mouths the flesh of their own children. They rip open the stomachs of others and stuff into the gaping wound the quartered body of the child whom the women recently carried in their arms.'

Once such atrocities were survived, a defensive determination was born that they would never occur again. Armenia can act the aggressor: an empire, after all, is always based on the successful waging of war. In 1990, after the splintering of the Soviet states, Armenia invaded the region of Karabagh, a province that despite having a predominantly Armenian population had belonged to Azerbaijan since 1918. It was a typical example of cynical manipulation of borders: only with the strong hand of the Soviet system could internal conflicts be discouraged.

The aggressive action of 1990 was interpreted in Yerevan as a justifiable reclamation of land, something strongly disputed in Azerbaijan. 'Karabagh has always been closely linked to Armenia,' said Naira Melkoumian, the Minister of Foreign Affairs for the newly established Republic of Karabagh. In Baku, you will hear a different story. Vafa Guluzade, Policy Adviser in Azerbaijan's Foreign Ministry, retorted, 'What Armenia did was nothing but an undiluted act of aggression. They were financed by the Russians.' The Azerbaijanis admit that there were many Armenians in the region, but Guluzade comments, 'There are also many Mexicans in California, it is true, but this does not take California out of America.'

What sets Armenia apart from the other nations of the Caucasus is her diaspora. There are Armenian populations in over seventy countries of the world, and the three million natives of Armenia are outnumbered by some eight million who live elsewhere. This is the heart of being Armenian: the willingness to adapt, the refusal to change. Wherever the seed falls, the same tree grows.

The diaspora has meant, however, that Armenians are phenomenally well connected. Their lobby in America is strong, as is their relationship to Russia. Guluzade claimed that 'Armenians are receiving American aid and aid from the Armenian diaspora – two hundred million dollars from the diaspora and one hundred million economic aid from the US, but Armenia is paying thirty to forty per cent of maintenance of Russian troops there – it is a ridiculous situation. American citizens are paying for Russian military bases in Armenia.'

While other countries have been forced to choose sides, Armenia negotiates a highwire that mirrors her tricky position in the Caucasus. The Armenian nation has long been vulnerable to attack from her Muslim neighbours, suffering at the hands of the powerful Ottoman and Persian empires. Yet, somehow, Armenia survives, the pressure merely making the country harder, more determined and very aware of her differences to her neighbours.

Various attempts are made to explain the complete lack of knowledge about Imam Shamil. 'We are not truly Caucasians,' says the philosopher. 'We are not even in the Caucasus,' stresses Ararat. The European influence is obvious, even among the shadows cast by the Soviet buildings of Yerevan. Everywhere there are people sipping coffee. Jazz cafés pour people on to the streets. We attend piano recitals, artists' studios, a modern dance rehearsal. Taran and John keep shaking their heads. After our time in the mountains, Ararat has provided an unexpected cultural shock.

All our enquiries into the recent past, the days of Imam Shamil, are greeted by shrugs. Men who know the entire histories of their nations, who quote Western philosophers at us, do not recognize his name. The historians at the local university seem to know, but in a lengthy and heated interview they refuse to discuss Imam Shamil. They are convinced that our interest is biased, that by investigating a Muslim figure we are ill-disposed to the history of their own country. Armenia was, after all, the first state in the world to adopt Christianity. Ancient churches cover the countryside, all shadowed by the snow-capped Mount Ararat. It looms over Armenia from within Turkey's borders, a daily reminder of salvation and a lost empire.

The professors even warn our host against us. 'You do not know who these people are,' stresses the older professor, 'you do not know them. You may find yourself in trouble if you are their host. How do you know what they want, how do you know what they will say after they have gone? You will still be here, but they have gone.'

Ararat is mildly shaken. At first, he questions us again of our intentions, then reverses his anger and aims it at the historians. Their thoughts, he says, are like leftovers of the Soviet mentality. Still, another problem has crept into the trip. Ararat's English is better than Ilya's, but he is shy with his skill. He confesses to us the following day that some of the questions we asked the historians were distorted by Ilya. Questions we had phrased with delicacy were ignored by our 'translator', who had decided to propose thornier, provocative questions. It helped explain our poor reception at the university.

It is testament to Ilya's strength of character that while a month ago such information would have caused great concern, now it just elicits exhausted shakes of the head. If we all began the journey orbiting Taran, it is now Ilya who is the source of gravity. It is most notable in the case of language. We all presumed, two months ago, that Ilya's English would improve throughout the journey. Instead, now we communicate in broken phrases. All of Ilya's catchphrases have been adopted: *Seven, twenty-four. He coming in, he no go out. Everything five by five. I fucking kill you.*

Back among friends in Ararat's house, even long, drunken dinners cannot stir memories of Shamil. 'We are Christian, the oldest Christians in the world,' insists the sculptor, 'we do not know of Imams.' Yet the connections between Shamil and Armenia do exist. The Chavchavadzes had a pair of estates in Armenia; Shamil's second wife was an Armenian; two of Russia's most successful generals in the Caucasus were Armenian; and, of course, Gramov, the go-between used by the negotiators, was Armenian.

# CHAPTER 20

# Towards Freedom

*The role of intermediary was perfectly suited to the thirty-two-year-old Gramov. He was not Russian, not affected by French culture like the St Petersburg officers, but was a reasonably undistinguished soldier. The very things that had made his nation vulnerable gave him his strengths. From Armenia's delicate geographic position, he had drawn his determination, from the mountains he had learned endurance, from the surrounding ethnicities he had grasped both customs and languages. He was described as having a 'quick, penetrating glance, and a laconic style of conversation, in which every thought appears to have been at once and finally cast in the most appropriate of words'. Above all, he had adapted his experiences into well-honed diplomacy. In the Caucasus, an area abounding in different customs, Gramov was the epitome of tact, a necessary skill to communicate between two parties so obsessed with force and pride.*

He was granted the job of negotiating the release of the hostages at the most sensitive time. After Chavchavadze's outburst, the talks were brittle and likely to end in disappointment for all sides. The true pressure was exerted neither by Shamil nor Chavchavadze, but by the Murid *naibs*, who saw this as a singular opportunity for profit. Enough money might be raised to continue the war against Russia for another thirty years and they were no longer afraid to whisper. They had found out that David Chavchavadze's brother-in-law was the Prince of Minghrelia. It was an honorary title, but was interpreted as a sign of further wealth and the demands increased accordingly.

Gramov's first foray into the mountains was notable for its consideration. They did not meet at Dargo, for Shamil was campaigning. The Armenian paused one kilometre from the Imam's tent and wrote Shamil a letter, asking him what he should wear during their meeting. Dressed as a Russian officer, Gramov entered the Imam's tent, the sound of battle carried in bursts by the wind. The first evening, they talked for almost an hour in Shamil's native tongue of Avar, and as Gramov later related, it was almost entirely an exchange of compliments. Having spent much time in the mountains, he was entirely used to this form of business. Hospitality was a serious task, the roles of guest and host so well defined that not even the most earnest of business might be hurried. Finally, Shamil asked, 'Will my son return to me?'

'You must know', returned Gramov, 'that your son has become half Russian.'

It is easy to see Gramov as direct, perhaps honest to a fault, but having worked in intelligence before, he was aware of Shamil's elaborate spy network and understood that he was only confirming what Shamil already knew. Still, with the skill of the diplomat, his delivery was tinged with hope.

'If he inherits your large views,' continued Gramov, 'he will certainly return. For it is better to command thousands here than mere hundreds in Russia.'

They spent the next three evenings drinking the better part of a brick of tea. It was a mountain mixture, a compote of sheep's blood and leaves that was neatly cut into solid cubes. The hostages were never mentioned, the favoured topics of conversation being the different generals that the Russians had sent to the Caucasus over the last twenty years. They talked of the other wars that Russia was involved in, Shamil peculiarly well informed of the Crimean theatre, often enquiring into the siege at Sebastopol.

The scene of the battle moved from day to day, and Shamil's tent and his negotiations with Gramov followed, the fighting often audible to the intermediary. Though Gramov calculated that the Murids were well beaten on the first day, never, he said, did Shamil show anything but utter composure. Once, when riding along a path, between the times of their formal negotiations, the Imam turned to Gramov and asked him what he thought of the roads in Dagestan and Chechnya.

'They are very bad, very dirty,' said Gramov. 'Travelling is rendered very difficult in your country, by the numerous woods, rivers and defiles. I only make seven miles a day and can say nothing favourable about my journey.'

Shamil appreciated his words. 'I am a common mountaineer,' he said, 'but these roads, the woods and mountains make me stronger than a great many monarchs. You see this horse,' continued Shamil, 'with two bags swung across its back?'

'Yes.'

'This is the way to go on a campaign. It is the whole of my baggage. It contains all I require on a march, and yet I am an Imam. With you, every ensign carries more. That is why your columns are so long: and you will agree with me that long straggling columns are not very desirable on a march.'

That night, the Imam pressed Gramov over the matter of the one million roubles. Without the *naibs* in attendance, Gramov spoke honestly.

'Even if the Chavchavadzes had one million roubles, the Tsar would not permit them to give such a sum to you. They know that it would be used to carry on the war.' He repeated Chavchavadze's offer of forty thousand, explaining that it was an extraordinary amount for one man to have raised.

Shamil listened. 'They write so much. It would be so much better to write less and do more.'

In Dargo, where Gramov had now scheduled his final meeting with Shamil before his return to the valleys, Zaidette believed that she had discovered the key to the princesses' weakness. She had informed them of the deadline imposed by David Chavchavadze and how they had three days of hope left before they were to be disowned by their families. She perfected the creation of a wicked vacillation between hope and despair for the captives. One day, she would announce that Jamal al-Din had finally reached the mountains, the next shake her head and say that without the million roubles they would remain for ever in the *aoul*.

Her recommendations were calculated to increase tension. 'Prince David must walk door to door throughout Georgia, asking for the money that you require from the people.' The captives' sole source of comfort, Shuanette, was cursed by Shamil's first wife for her kindness. 'You are not really Muslim,' shouted Zaidette at Shuanette. 'You are offending both Mohammed and your husband. You cannot be trusted.' Both the princesses and Madame Drancy were too proud to cry in front of their captors, but once the door was closed for the night, the women began to sob.

The last meeting between Gramov and Shamil took place in the Imam's quarters in Dargo. They sat patiently amid a gaggle of boisterous *naibs*, who remained intent on obtaining every rouble of the proposed million. Gramov saw no point in trying to dissuade them and waited until the prayer call broke up their meeting. Alone with Shamil, he was asked by the Imam to give an honest opinion of their situation. Gramov suggested that Shamil should be happy with the position that he had forced his enemies into. 'It will not be a small thing to be able to boast that you compelled the Russians to restore your son, whom the Tsar treasured as his own. The whole world will hear of this.'

Shamil nodded. 'It will be well to receive the money, too.'

For one last time, the patient Gramov explained the impossibility of obtaining more than forty thousand roubles.

'So be it,' said Shamil.

Gramov knew that the Imam's problem was not one of greed, but a trickier proposition of keeping his own lieutenants satisfied with his actions. He wanted nothing more than his son, yet could not lose face among the Murids. Shamil began to write a letter to David Chavchavadze in front of Gramov. It began, 'Money is grass. It withers and is gone. We do not serve money but God.' The words boded well, but both men had seen so many letters pass back and forth between the mountains and the lowlands that neither presumed it the end of the matter.

Even inside the seraglio, the princesses and Madame Drancy were aware of the awkwardness of the Imam's position. That night Shamil entered the mosque, knowing that in the morning the *naibs* would gather once more to hear his final decision on the matter of the ransom. Rumours leaked through to the princesses. Some of the *naibs* were begging the Imam to sell the women. Others were trying to convince him that the man brought to the fort from

St Petersburg was not his son, Jamal al-Din, but a stranger; that his son had died in Tbilisi of cholera; that the Russians had poisoned him.

Shamil's answer was inspired, showing that even in such tortuous times, when his thoughts must have spun around the return of his son, he was still capable of a diplomatic sleight of hand. With the *naibs* gathered before him, he announced that it was not a decision he was capable of making, for the matter of Jamal al-Din clouded his head. Instead, he referred the question to a hermitical holy man, known throughout the mountains for his wisdom and habit of living in total solitude. There seems little doubt that Shamil sent word before him. The hermit was brought to Dargo that night, where he performed for the *naibs*, howling, praying, crying, joined by all the women of the *aoul*, so that the princesses and Madame Drancy were kept from sleep by the feverish noises. All the *naibs* responded to such a display of religious fervour, swaying in similar febrile states, so that when the old man announced his decision the next morning, the *naibs* could not contradict the word of Allah.

'Do not imitate the infidels,' declared the old man, 'who revel in luxury and whose women offend Allah with their ways of flattery and deceit. Renounce everything that comes from Russia, both tea and sugar and all their luxuries. Do not keep these women, but chase them from here, they are our enemies. Do not ask for a million roubles, but return them to their country so the Imam might receive his son from the Tsar.' An agreement had been reached, and word was sent down to where Jamal al-Din and David Chavchavadze waited.

The feelings inside the seraglio were extraordinarily mixed. Madame Drancy admits that during the long eight months they had built up a certain fondness for the customs of the *aoul*, and a liking for the call to prayer. The final days were spent as David

Chavchavadze gathered the money in silver. Shamil would not take gold, most likely because such a large amount of silver would make a better impression on the people, and also be more easily divided between his *naibs*. In Dargo, Shamil prepared a house for Jamal al-Din, then gave Avar costumes to the little Georgian princes.

When the time came to take their leave, the captives visited Shuanette one last time and found her sick, lying on a carpet by a fire. Even in poor health, Shuanette professed her happiness for their release. Madame Drancy could not help herself, but began to cry, thinking of all of the kindness the Imam's wife had offered them over the months. Zaidette shook them all by the hand and begged them to remember how they had always been treated as members of her family. Princess Anna replied, with great diplomacy, that they would forget neither kindnesses nor those who had offered them. All the captives were given veils so that no man might look upon them during their journey to freedom. It was a damp March day and the princesses, their children and charges and Madame Drancy sat in rough carts. Finally, they were pulled from the gates of Dargo.

Horsemen gathered about them, and it was only when the carts rolled on to open ground that the Frenchwoman was able to estimate the numbers. She reckoned that they were escorted by seven thousand men. They began to chant, a call and response sweeping from one side of the army to the other, singing songs in honour of Shamil and Jamal al-Din. Rifles and pistols were fired into the air. Shamil rode past them, wearing a long green tunic over his familiar white *shouba*. Madame Drancy wrote that 'his face radiated joy, his heart was doubly happy both to see his favourite son and to return the women to their families'. As he passed, he paused and picked up one of the young Georgian princes for a last embrace.

After two nights, they arrived at the top of a hill. Shamil's chief steward, Khadji, pointed across a small river beneath them and said,

'There is the Russian army.' Madame Drancy said that those simple words acted as a shock. Before them lay an entire encampment and, away from the Russians, a vast tent, in which the final negotiations would take place. Khadji galloped forward. Inside the bags strapped to his horse was a full set of native clothes for Jamal al-Din.

The last night of captivity was spent with the two vast forces on either side of the river. After midnight, Isaac Gramov was surprised to find himself awoken by a mountaineer. He was informed that his presence was requested by Shamil. Gramov was shaken, filled with sudden doubts that the complex negotiations that he had patiently coordinated would be once again enmeshed. He took a stiff tumbler of punch, made the sign of the cross and left. Shamil was simply anxious and greeted Gramov warmly.

'My Isaac Beg has nearly been frozen on the road,' said Shamil to one of his attendants, as the order was dispatched to bring boiling tea. 'I wanted to see you,' continued Shamil, 'in order to thank you for the services you have rendered me. I know all. You went to meet my son, were constantly with him, and behaved very well. Second, tomorrow is a great day for us. Tomorrow we shall be at peace with the Russians and there must be no foul play . . . where great persons are concerned, good faith cannot be too well observed.'

This was merely a preamble. At the heart of Gramov's visit was the desire of a father to know more about the son he had not seen in fifteen years.

'I am told that he does not speak a word of Avar.'

'That is true,' answered Gramov, 'but it is natural enough. He has lived so many years in Russia. You must not find fault with him on that account. When he has been with you some time, he will speak it again.'

'Believe me, I shall let him live just as he likes. Only let him live with me . . . I cannot sleep at night for thinking of him. Only let the affair be terminated without treachery.'

They talked, propped on pillows, until six in the morning. Shamil was particularly amused that after eight months of fighting in Sebastopol the city had still not been taken. 'After that,' he said, 'I may be justly proud of holding out against the Russian armies.'

The next morning thirty-five men from either side rode with their respective prisoners towards a lone tree by the side of the Mitchik River. Shamil's steward, Khadji, rode beside the Imam, holding a large black parasol above his head. The prisoners were greeted by David Chavchavadze and a smattering of Russian generals. Jamal al-Din stepped forward, and with the manners of a Russian tea party politely excused himself to the women for not having arrived sooner.

The Russian and Georgian regiments filled the air with their songs. Salutes were exchanged between the generals of the armies. Jamal al-Din and David Chavchavadze shook hands. Then the latter opened his arms for a moment, and they were filled with his happy children. The princesses were still wearing the veils that they had been issued in the seraglio. When, finally, they pulled them off, there was no celebration. Instead, reported Princess Anna, she had the curious feeling that she had seen her husband only the day before.

The captives caught up on news, and little of it was good. The day that Tsinondali had been burned to the ground, Princess Orbeliani's father had died suddenly. That Christmas, in France, Madame Drancy's mother had been taken by cholera. Tsar Nicholas, who had engineered their release, was buried on 11 March, the very same day that the prisoners were exchanged. It was a strange series of events, as if the true ransom was not forty thousand roubles, but the passing of a generation.

While for Madame Drancy the sight of the Russian army settled in the plain beneath had signalled to her the end of her captivity, Anna Chavchavadze was not affected emotionally until dinner that night. It was only after she had seen the care with which her husband had lined the table, ensuring that her favourite dishes lay before her, that she realized that life had changed once more. David Chavchavadze lit a cigarette. As he exhaled, his wife breathed in the smoke and only then did she begin to cry for all she had suffered.

There must have been a brief hope that Jamal al-Din would represent a communion between the two warring countries. As he took his leave of the princes and princesses, a Russian baron handed him his own sabre as a gift.

'Do not cut at any of our people with it,' he said with a smile.

'Neither yours nor ours,' answered the young man.

He directed his horse towards the main force of Murids. They could no longer contain themselves and Jamal al-Din and his small escort of Cossacks were swamped by the joyful mountaineers. A Prussian officer who witnessed the scene commented that the tribesmen kept trying 'to kiss Jamal al-Din's hand, the hem of his tunic, his boots . . . he submitted very quietly'. Khadji rode forward with the clothes he had carried from Dargo.

Shamil refused to greet his son while he still wore the uniform of a Russian officer. For the sake of Jamal al-Din's civilized sensibilities, the Murids formed a tight circle about him, so that no one could see him while he stripped. When the sea of Murids parted, Jamal al-Din stood alone, wearing a long black *tcherkesska*, his head topped by a lambskin *papakh*. He remounted his horse and rode to his father. The Murid hordes broke into wild cries. As Jamal al-Din neared Shamil, the din quietened. When father embraced son, all noted that Shamil was in tears. But it was only when Jamal al-Din turned to his fellow officers for his final goodbye that *he* began to weep.

The Murids spent the day counting every one of the silver roubles, not because they feared being short-changed, but because they were frightened of being overpaid and that the Russians would later use this as a pretext to challenge the validity of the exchange. Before retreating to Dargo, Shamil sent once more for Gramov and told him, 'I value your services highly. My children and all my family will ever remember them. If you, or any of your relatives, should fall into our hands, know that you will instantly be freed . . . At present I have nothing with me to offer you in remembrance of me; but I will send you something, which I hope you will accept.' The Imam kept his word, and a few weeks later one of Shamil's emissaries sought out the Armenian, presenting him with a watch set in diamonds, worth almost six hundred roubles.

Jamal al-Din's journey into the mountains was marked by the hope that perhaps he might find traces of his childhood self. Both he and his father would be disappointed by the impossibility of such an act of reclamation.

From recent information, it appears that Jamal al-Din has already accomplished a journey around and through the territory over which his father reigned . . . In military affairs he never intervenes. He is allowed to write occasionally to his friends in Russia, upon the condition that his letters are not too long. From some of these letters we have ascertained that the mountaineers continually assure him he was very fortunate to get away from Russia. Jamal al-Din does not believe this; but he remains silent, and remembers the Russian proverb, 'If you live with wolves, you must howl with them.'

The tone of optimism in this extract from the *Kavkaz* newspaper, August 1856, was entirely misplaced. Jamal al-Din was married to the young daughter of a *naib*, then sent deep into the mountains, far from the temptations of the border lands. His efforts to keep his spirits up soon suffered. Virtually from the moment he greeted his father, his health declined. Despite frequent trips by emissaries to doctors in the lowlands, Jamal al-Din died of tuberculosis within two years of the hostage exchange.

# CHAPTER 21

# Tours and Travels

*Small countries with long histories are well-marked lands. Events are spread over such a limited area that memories are stacked in the same location again and again, like storeys of a building. Armenia gives the impression of being much larger, its canyons, mountains, lakes, rivers and extinct volcanoes making all roads curve and all drives long.*

Armenia even claims to have been the birthplace of humanity. Her church places the Garden of Eden near the Euphrates and Tigris, with the headwaters at Lake Van, within Armenia's historical borders. Perhaps, it is theorized, the garden lies in her depths. More appealing is a game of etymology. 'Edin', in Sumeri, means a 'steppe' or 'terrace', while 'paradise' in Farsi can be divided between *pairi* ('around') and *daeza* ('walls') – thus Eden becomes a fortified stockade. This at least is more Caucasian, leaving the Garden of Eden always out of reach, sitting atop the next mountainous horizon. It would be a shame to leave it under an inland sea.

Noah's Ark, on the other hand, is easier to place. Most agree that should it be discovered anywhere, then it would be where the Bible specified: on Mount Ararat. Ararat, our host, keeps a telescope on the balcony of his studio and keeps insisting that on clear days it is easy to spot the Ark. There have been two eye-witness accounts of the Ark, the first of which was given by a ten-year-old boy in 1910. He and his uncle were out walking on Ararat and, according to the story, the uncle fired bullets off the Ark to demonstrate its toughness. He hoisted the small boy on to the roof of the Ark; the boy knelt and kissed it, then explored the ship's many empty chambers.

In 1916 a Russian pilot, Lieutenant Roskovitsky, spotted the submerged hull of a huge ship as he flew above a half-frozen lake on the higher slopes of the mountain. He noted a pair of masts and a catwalk traversing a wooden roof. Later in the day, he flew his captain over the same site to confirm his findings. A 150-man expedition was sent out to find the Ark. They took measurements and photographs that unfortunately were destroyed by Leon Trotsky after the Communists seized power. Or so the story went, when published by *New Eden Magazine* in 1939. It ran on news wires for a year, until the magazine's shamefaced editor confessed to fabricating the entire tale. However, though unable to find it again, the young boy who had clambered about the Ark did pass a lie-detector test. Still, his findings are contradicted by Genesis, in chapter 8, verse 13, where it is specified that Noah had removed the roof. Whatever the young boy was kissing, it is unlikely that it was Noah's Ark.

Under Ararat and under all of Armenia run a series of fault lines. The largest of recent earthquakes, in 1988, left fifty thousand dead and one of her oldest cities, Gyumri, demolished. Of all arts in Armenia, it is unsurprising, then, that an added importance is placed on architecture. Over the centuries, bridges, caravanserais and fortresses have fallen to the shaking earth. Yet many of Armenia's earliest churches have survived, as if only secular constructions were predestined to crumble. All the churches were built entirely in stone, almost always from the volcanic tufa that is available across the country in shades of red, pink, orange or black. It is lightweight material, easy to sculpt and gradually hardening over time. Mortar was made from shattered pieces of tufa, lime, broken stones and eggs. The churches, then, were essentially made of the same materials as the ground that they stood on, making them share, but not cede to, the struggles of the earth.

Dead empires tend to breed an intense patriotism and, if anything, this is what ties Armenia to the rest of the Caucasus. Having parents from different countries I am, by nature, unpatriotic, never wanting to side too far against half my blood. Ilya is a Turkman, who grew up in Uzbekistan and has lived for years in places as diverse as New York and Siberia. Amid such confusion, he relies on his religion to identify himself. When he is asked where he's from he always answers, 'I am a Jew.' Taran's answers are even more confounding, once identifying himself as Welsh, American, English, Jewish and Christian within the space of a day. This always makes John, a staunch New Englander, laugh aloud. We are a strange collection, but perhaps none of us has ever lived anywhere long enough to foster the kind of pride that is taken for granted in the Caucasus.

To Taran's eternal disgruntlement, a guidebook to Azerbaijan was published the very month we arrived in the Caucasus. The fact that I appeared with a copy was a mixed blessing. Now we knew where we were going, even when we suspected that the writer hadn't been there himself, but it also tarnished the novelty factor, effectively turning travel into tourism. Since Taran is a member of the Explorers' Club in New York this was a grievous wound and the core of many arguments, where any posturing was forever undermined by the evil red book.

Taran would wait until we were in the most remote and

beautiful spot, take a seat, share a warm beer, then say, 'Are you a traveller or a tourist?'

'Tourist.'

'Why?'

'What's a traveller?'

'It's about the way you see it,' Taran would begin. 'Do you travel with others, on buses, staying safe, eating Western food, living in Western accommodation? Or do you live with locals, eat with them, drink with them? The difference between travel and tourism is the way you approach a country.'

'So when faced with two options,' I ask, 'being a traveller is about selecting the uncomfortable choice?'

'Fine,' says Taran, 'you can be a tourist.'

'Fine.'

While drinking, those participating regress to the age that they met. In Taran's and my case, this is thirteen, which is why I continue to needle him. 'What about the flag?'

Taran was proud of the flag. Quite rightly so, for the Explorers' Club had sponsored trips to the moon, to the depths of the ocean, to the tops of the Himalayas. The very flag we carried had been planted on the highest peak in the Caucasus eighty years ago. But in fairness, our journey was a trail, and trails necessarily mean that you are following in someone's path. In this case, a fairly well-trodden path. Even Taran admitted that we weren't exactly explorers. He shakes his head. He may be proud of the flag, but is uncomfortable with the fact that it was Ilya who had carried it to its intended destination in Dagestan. It was a low blow to bring it up.

'Forget about the flag,' Taran says with a smile.

'How about the guidebook?' asks John, and laughter begins again.

# CHAPTER 22

# Driven from the Mountains

*Thirty years after Veliamenov had written that the Caucasus could only be taken slowly, never by the quick, decisive thrusts that had cost the Russian infantry so heavily, did the tacticians pay heed. With the Treaty of Paris signed in 1856, Russia was free to turn her considerable manpower on the stubborn mountaineers. The matter was simple enough. Every victory that Shamil had earned over the last thirty years had allowed the population to forget about their considerable losses. The answer to how the Russians might avoid losing again was simple enough: do not fight.*

'Fighting', noted Prince Bariatinsky, Tsar Alexander's new commander in the Caucasus, 'implies some sort of equality, and so long as they could fight, the enemy had no thought of submission. But when, time after time, they found that, in fact, they could never come to blows, their weapons fell from their hands. Beaten, they would have gathered again on the morrow. Shamil's power is being undermined by nothing so much as fruitless gatherings of men who had to disperse to their homes without anywhere offering serious defence.'[13]

Perhaps the greatest symbol of Shamil's waning power in the Caucasus was the Argoun Forest. For many years, Russians would simply avoid it. So tall and thick were its trees that it was considered impregnable. Yet, in 1858, after a two-pronged push against Chechen positions, the forest was finally taken. This forward movement was achieved not through battle and bloodshed, but by the painstaking clearing of the trees.

As Baddeley said, 'As long as these forests stood, the Chechens were unconquerable. The Russians made no permanent impression on them save when and where they cut the beech trees down; and it is literally the fact that they were beaten in the long run not by the sword but by the axe.'[14]

The mountaineers were no different from their land. It is neither a metaphor nor a symbol but simply a fusion between man and his terrain. Veliamenov had faced trees so large and swarming with the enemy that he had compared each trunk to a fort. General Grabbe had experienced rock slides and desolate wasteland. General Freitag encountered human boulders. The fallen beech trees that blocked Vorontsov were intermeshed with branches and inhabited by Chechens. Everywhere they faced man and nature together.

Perhaps the most powerful image was that which greeted the Karbada regiment on the third day of the Biscuit Expedition: the barricades that stood before them, the fallen beech trees reinforced by the naked and mutilated corpses of their fellow Russian soldiers. These hybrid bulwarks of flesh and wood stand as a wretched symbol of Caucasian warfare. Shamil had long understood that the countryside provided more pragmatic assistance than Allah. Any man who felled a tree was first penalized an ox. At the second offence he would be punished with death, the same penalty as either cowardice or treachery, underlining the importance of the land. The body would hang in the centre of the man's *aoul* for at least one week.

Shamil even used metaphors concerning nature when exhorting his Murids. After a morale threatening defeat, the Imam preached, 'When the lightning strikes one tree, do all the others bow their heads and cast themselves down, lest it strike them also? Oh, ye of little faith, would that ye might take example from the green wood.' During one of Shamil and Isaac Gramov's long conversations, the Imam declared, 'I ought to anoint all my trees with oil, and to mix the mud of my roads with fragrant honey.' Shamil may have been the most devout of Muslims, but such animist statements appealed both to his Murids and the people.

Few Russians were willing to understand this. Tolstoy and Lermontov might have seen the wonder of the mountains, and the bravery of the men who inhabited them, but few were struck by the solution: the only way to silence Shamil was not by defeating his men but by taming his land. It would never be a matter of glory. There would be no cavalry charges, rearguard actions or protracted sieges that would directly result in the fall of Shamil. Instead, Chechnya would be conquered by the endless swing of axes, tree after tree creaking, leaning and crashing through the undergrowth as it fell to the forest floor.

During the summer of 1858, the Argoun Forest had been cleared of a large swathe of her ancient trees. So great had the Russian fear of the forest been that those stationed in remoter forts refused to believe that such a mission had now been completed. The news filtered through the men, the officers, even to their wives. The women were insistent that they should view this place that had held so much terror for their husbands. Soon ponies and traps sped along the lines, carrying women and picnics into the dread forest. The day was spent peering into the well-defended gloom, laughing. Their picnic tables were the stumps of trees. Dediamenov, a Russian officer, wrote to a friend,

> Thousands of carts belonging to the 'peaceful' Chechens were requisitioned to carry away the timber; the inhabitants of Vozdvizhenskoe hastened out to buy it and sell their own produce, or whatever was wanted by the troops; shops were opened, and booths set up by vendors of goods and drink and every sort of petty trader. In a word, the gloomy, wild and inaccessible defile acquired in a very short time the busy aspect of a vast and varied market, people everywhere, crowds of buyers and sellers, and on all sides long lines of carts laden with different commodities.[15]

The transition from the Chechen connection to land to the Russian absorption of it was almost complete. The aim of empire, in the Russian case, was to make the wilds of Chechnya look like the well-tamed southern steppes. In one swift move, the forest had gone from fortress to tradable asset. The language Dediamenov uses is extraordinary. Within a paragraph he uses the words, 'buy', 'produce', 'sell', 'shops', 'vendors', 'traders', 'markets' and 'commodities'. Shamil had dismissed money, but the Russian style of economics was now in practice less than twenty miles from Dargo.

Why, then, did the Chechens along the edges of the Argoun not fight these invaders? Shamil had not descended with his thousands of troops. Without encouragement, the locals were absurdly outnumbered. The Russians were able to mass close to Dargo. In this one area, they deployed forty thousand men and forty-eight field guns. Once news of such a force had spread, its number, combined with sheer exhaustion from thirty years of warfare, made the prospect of any kind of peace welcome.

Trees kept falling. Three separate columns were hewing their way through woods towards Dargo. Some of the beech trees were measured at almost three hundred feet in height and thirty-five feet in diameter. There was no time to drag them from the forests. Often, they were either burned or dynamited, until finally a tree-less stretch almost a mile wide reached all the way to the right bank of the Argoun River, six thousand feet above sea level. From this position, it was possible to see the *aoul* of Dargo, less than ten miles away. By now, the only guns employed by the Russians were used to defend the working parties. Axemen and dynamiters were guarded by regiments spread in thick lines about them.

If nature had granted Shamil a stronghold, she was also responsible for the original division of tribes that were now splintering under Russian pressure. Baddeley, after riding through the stretch of mountains, concluded that 'It may be said, without exaggeration, that the mountains made the men; and the men in return fought with passionate courage and energy in defence of their beloved mountains, in whose fastness, indeed, they were well-nigh unconquerable.'[16]

These were, however, the same mountains that had always separated tribe from tribe, such harsh terrain that entire language groups could coexist within a few miles of one another. The wonder of the histories of the Caucasus could be found in the Adats. Their beauty was that, unlike Shamil's interpretation of the Sharia, they changed from village to village, generous interpretations making allowances for the differences that marked one mountain from another.

Both Shamil and the Russians sought to force forms of state administration on *aouls* that had always been dictated by family structures. The greatest irony of all was that, in order to defend the Caucasus, Shamil began to impose an administrative network and state machine that were perfectly suited to the Russian concepts of centralized rule.

The dwindling Murids had little option but to gather at Dargo. Their last mistake, guaranteed to turn the local populations against them, was to burn all the surrounding *aouls* to keep their stores from falling into Russian hands. Such fanaticism, when it was already obvious to the native villagers that the Murid cause was lost, resulted in a sudden switch of allegiance. In rare cases, the Chechens even rose up against the Murids, turning them from *aouls*, then sending messages to inform the Russians of their deeds. One last attempt was made by the Imam to take the offensive. Responding to a miniature uprising in the plains, he rushed down under artillery fire to turn the spark into fire, but received only heavy casualties and was driven back to Dargo. How much had the Russians learned? That day they had killed 370 Murids for the loss of only 16 of their own men.

With winter snows preventing the encirclement of Dargo, the Russians patiently kept the forests at bay and the roads clear so that when the spring of 1859 arrived, they might move immediately. A two-month siege, begun when snows were still heavy in the mountains, resulted in the loss of Dargo. Shamil had not stayed, but fled south. Since 1839 he had made his home in Chechnya, but now, at the time of greatest need, he returned to Dagestan.

Yevdokimov, known throughout the Caucasus as the Three-Eyed General (thanks to a scar between his eyes), pursued the Imam hard. As Shamil's *naibs* tried to gather their forces, Russian agents were simultaneously attempting to convert opposing *aouls* into groups of militia. It resulted in partial success. Shamil's own train was attacked by the village of Akhvakh. It was an *aoul* famed for its savagery, its inhabitants known for their penchant for raw meat. Still, it was not an act of understandable defection, but outright treachery coupled with aggression. Such betrayal must have made the desperation of his position even more obvious to Shamil.

Gounib, however, remained loyal, though Shamil's entire force now numbered only four hundred men. On 25 August, the Russian assault began. Morning in the mountains is an extraordinary sight: clouds roll backwards, peeling themselves from the rock, then fade into the sun like winter breath. Within the first hour of the battle, as swarms of Russian infantry rose from these smoky mists, 350 Murids died, including a body of 100 who had fought to the last man. Without the consideration of his family, there can be little doubt that Shamil would have imitated so many of his followers. Instead, he sent a pair of emissaries to sue for peace.

Once again, it was an Armenian, Colonel Lazaroff, who conducted the negotiations, though they were simple enough: unconditional surrender or death. As Shamil rode from the gates of Gounib, he was greeted not with the familiar yells of his Murids, but by the roar of forty thousand Russians, relieved that at last they had captured the Imam. Shamil is said to have wheeled his horse about, horrified again by his submission and determined to resume the slaughter. Lazaroff grasped his reins and quickly explained that in Russia this was a signal of honour for an opposing sultan. The commander, Prince Bariatinsky, sat waiting for the Imam on a stone. He rose at Shamil's approach and accepted the Imam's sword, saying that he would answer for the safety of his family. All else would depend on the Tsar.

The very things that had carried the Imam upwards had now dragged him down. The imposition of such a strict doctrine upon a largely animist people was a yoke that many looked forward to breaking. The mountains were always a land of splintered stars and differing tongues, and while the blanket of Islam may have covered the cracks of unshared customs, thirty years of unceasing warfare had exhausted all. This was not a thought alien to Shamil, who commented that it was he who had made the Caucasus conquerable. It was he who had formed the coalitions under the Sharia, a shadow of the state control that the Russians were soon to manifest.

Had the mountaineers been free to read the press of St Petersburg, they would have been shocked that a second appropriation of their range was being conducted, this time in print. The works of Pushkin, Lermontov and Tolstoy had seized the Russian imagination. The great Caucasian range had been transformed from a place where the mountaineers drew strength to a source of inspiration for Russian novelists and poets. Olenin, Tolstoy's protagonist in *The Cossacks*, sees the Caucasus rise before him and feels nothing less than liberation. '*Abreks* canter about the plain, and here am I driving along and do not fear them! I have a gun, and strength, and youth . . . and the mountains.' It is interesting to note that thirty years later, when Tolstoy wrote *Hadji Murad*, his view of the mountains was much more muted.

There is no better place than the wilderness for a civilized country to measure its customs. As the land is rich in minerals, waiting to add to the wealth of the conqueror, so its inhabitants are incorporated into the culture, on the victor's terms. Lermontov's dreams of galloping across gorges, wooing dark-eyed local beauties, made the Caucasus an exotic possibility that lurked on the edge of the Russian empire. Even within Russian experience in the Caucasus, the angles of approach began to change. Pushkin's declaration of Russian empire, calling for the mountain range to bow before Russian generals, gave way to Lermontov's romanticism, an adventurous enthusiasm that resulted in death, both for character and author. It is only with Tolstoy's last work, *Hadji Murad*, that a more realistic approach is taken.

In a scene that would be played out again and again in the coming century in Chechnya, Tolstoy has his captain send a report of an engagement between his soldiers and a band of local Chechens. It reads:

> 23rd Nov. Two companies of the Kurin regiment advanced from the fort on a wood-felling expedition. At midday a considerable number of mountaineers suddenly attacked the wood fellers. The sharpshooters began to retreat, but the 2nd company charged with the bayonet and overthrew the mountaineers. In this affair two privates were slightly wounded and one killed. The mountaineers lost about a hundred men.

It is a remarkable passage only because of the chapters that press either side of the report. The engagement mentioned is experienced some pages before by the reader, who thus knows that the action consisted of a brief exchange of five shots, resulting in no Chechen deaths whatsoever. Moreover, it was an ambitious captain who had put his men into such a dangerous position in the first place. The last view that Tolstoy gives of the episode is from the eyes of the dying Russian soldier. There is little to be pitied in the man, he is covered in scars received in a deserved whipping incurred for drinking away company money. He dies slowly, a clenched candle in his hand, dictating a letter. A surgeon pokes about, trying to extract the bullet. Tolstoy kills not only his Russian everyman, but soon enough his hero, Hadji Murad. There is no romance left, only a muted rejection of command and young hopes. Using the same subject matter with which as a young man Tolstoy had carved a romantic homage to the mountains, the writer in his final years finds a cynicism stunning for the directness of its anti-imperialism.

In the summer of 1860, Shamil saw his first train. Standing on the platform, watching this horseless wagon, tons of iron moving at speeds exceeding his fastest horses, the Imam must have wondered what exactly he had been fighting against. Russia was not a world of rock and wood, river and rain, but wires and metals, bulging with inventions that he had never dreamed of. And this was the very edge of the Tsar's empire.

During his progress towards St Petersburg the Imam was unsure of what would happen to him, expecting always to be torn to pieces by the enemy he had hounded for thirty years. At best, he imagined a fate similar to that of Vercingetorix. Like Shamil, the Gaul had retired to a stronghold. The Romans, familiar in the arts of siege warfare, formed a double circle of defence that was never penetrated. The captured Gaul was taken to Rome, where he participated in Caesar's triumph, and was summarily executed.

Both Shamil and his wives were given new clothes, the Imam outfitted at a military tailor's. By the time he reached the town of Kourtoumkali, Shamil had become even more puzzled. The officers' wives rode out to greet him with garlands. Why was he met as a victor? Was this the manner of a Russian triumph? Was he to be kept alive only until the Tsar might see him? At the town of Kharkov they were met with the news that the Tsar was near and wished Shamil's company for a review of his troops. On the road to meet the Tsar, a local colonel answered questions of concern. Shamil and his entourage, explained the colonel, were now in a Christian state, where forgiveness, meekness and patience brought their own rewards. Shamil may not have believed this or it may have confused him. He had fought the Russians for so long, seen atrocities committed by his enemy, ordered such atrocities himself. What, then, were the differences of this flat land, away from the mountains, where peace reigned inside the borders of the Russian empire? Exactly how diametric was this world?

The Tsar greeted Shamil during a parade of lancers. 'I am happy that you are here in Russia. We shall be friends.' Together, they spent the afternoon watching military manoeuvres and, by reported accounts, talked pleasantly for hours. Any remaining apprehension that Shamil had felt about the treatment of his family dissipated. They had been received in honour. Thousands of troops massed before him, cavalry coordinating in intricate patterns of exhibition, just a small sample of the numbers the Tsar had at his disposal.

A further surprise awaited Shamil. The following evening, he was granted an audience with the infamous General Yermolov. This brace of retired despots sat for hours, remembering their battles, a pair of ageing warriors in communion.

Another portrait of Shamil has been left behind, to add to Madame Drancy's and the princesses' accounts, by a Captain Runovsky, appointed by the Tsar as the Imam's adjutant. Speaking several mountain dialects, Runovsky was an observant man, forever smoothing the Imam's path through his strange transition into gilded captivity. Their first meeting, conducted along lines of competing compliments, brought them to an immediate understanding and began a firm friendship.

'The Tsar has appointed you as my adjutant,' said Shamil to Runovsky, 'but I believe Allah sent you . . . I promise you that I shall love you both as a grateful child, and as Shamil loves a man who is good to him.'

'I shall love you', replied Runovsky, 'not because I am ordered to do so, but because I respect you greatly.'

In the following week, as the two men passed through the busy streets of St Petersburg, the Imam and his entourage would often be subjected to a trail of idolizers and curious onlookers. Their enthusiasm still puzzled Shamil.

'Your men are pleased to see me a prisoner, yet they do not

wish me harm,' said Shamil, eyeing a growing crowd of admirers. 'With us it would be different. Our men would have stoned me – killed me. I shall write to the Caucasus and tell them to change their ways – to forbid our former violence; they will obey me, I think. Tell them', he said to Runovsky, while pointing to the sympathetic onlookers, 'that my feelings are as deep as my wounds. Tell them their attentions give me such happiness as I have not had since the liberation of Dargo.'

Shamil's last memories of his brief sojourn in St Petersburg were brightened by his first sight of photographs. The portraits of the Imam and his sons brought howls of joy from his remaining *naibs* who had followed Shamil into captivity. Even more pleasure was drawn from several visits to the zoological gardens. Many of the animals surprised the Imam in their strange manners, but none delighted him as much as the monkeys. He would sit and shake their hands, explaining to Runovsky that they were Jews who had angered God. All attempts to persuade him that they were monkeys were repelled with a discreet look of certainty.

The Moscow suburb of Kaluga was selected by the Tsar for Shamil's permanent refuge. It was a familiar Russian landscape: low fences, tree-lined streets, some houses simple, some displaying city airs of affectation. A dull provincial town, Kaluga was slowly expanding around its train station. For some time, the newness of experience kept the ache for the crags of Dagestan from the hearts of Shamil and his family.

Runovsky's weekly reports were sent immediately to Tsar Alexander in St Petersburg, and with such a perfect triangular rapport, the Tsar was able to surprise Shamil by granting wishes the Imam barely knew he had made. Thus, looks of admiration cast by the Imam or his sons at a well-bred horse resulted in the gift of a carriage and several stallions. Many of the transitions were more prosaic, such as the night scene at the dinner table. Runovsky reported that, 'The Murids made desperate efforts to catch mayonnaise on their forks, but found it quite unmanageable. At first, they were angry, but presently they gambled happily, licking their fingers, leaving their forks severely alone. Shamil looked at them with a slight air of superiority and made a few deprecating remarks on their clumsiness.'

The first two years of Shamil's captivity included short journeys to the estates of both the Tsar and Prince Bariatinsky. It was the closest taste to freedom that the mountaineers would ever have again: fine horses beneath them, breaking into a gallop, the illusion of independence reached with the gathering speed of their mounts. What these men shared, from Russian generals to adjutants, from Shamil to his youngest *naib*, was experience in war. Always, the conversation reverted to battles, or the state of the Russian army, or the Tsar's intentions at the edges of his empire.

Back in Kaluga, the novelty of change was evaporating, and was slowly replaced by an insidious desire by a select few for assimilation. Khadji, Shamil's faithful steward, was now devoted to colognes and provincial dances. He had managed to convince the Imam that if Shamil would not attend these functions, then he should at least send a representative as a sign of respect. Both Zaidette and Shuanette coveted the dresses of visitors and smuggled in the finest cloth, which Shamil later destroyed in anger. For the first year, Shamil had been reluctant to judge his new neighbours, attending balls, albeit sitting soberly on sofas, holding court among the infidels. But soon his intense dislike of luxury began to separate his house from the others in Kaluga. Gifts of gold or silver services were politely returned; wooden spoons were favoured at his table.

When Runovsky was replaced by an ill-tempered Pole, Shamil's position in the town became less comfortable. The straitjacket of provincial life became a little tighter. Shamil still considered himself the Tsar's guest, and remained grateful for all that Russia had done for his family. 'A man', he said, 'must never show displeasure at anything whatever, therefore I am generally satisfied.' Somehow, Shamil lived within this paradox. The Russia that had conquered his land, burned *aouls*, slaughtered families was now a different beast, showing magnanimity in victory, offering peace to his family. Often the Imam would be found staring across the outskirts of town: life was not controlled by him, nor even by the Tsar, but by Allah. 'The Caucasus is now here, in Kaluga,' he would say.

During his captivity, Shamil must finally have been able to see the truth of the strange dualities that his eldest son, Jamal al-Din, had also experienced. His next two sons swore an oath of allegiance to the Tsar in 1866, and the younger of the two was not only accepted into the military, but so well trusted that he was sent to the Caucasus to aid in the selection of native cavalry. It was at this time that Shamil became acquainted with the Chukin family, who had been the first to care for Jamal al-Din during the early years of his captivity. They had a boy of a similar age, who had been Jamal al-Din's best friend. The Imam would sit quietly and listen to the mother relate tales from his son's childhood; he did not like to talk after their visits.

While for his *naibs*, his wives and his sons Shamil's continued existence was the focus of their lives, the ageing Imam sought peace from above. He had found a translation of the Bible and was particularly intrigued by discovering the similarities between the book of Christian faith and his own Koran. In his life, devoted to his interpretation of the Sharia, there was only one ideal left to be attained: he had not yet completed the Hadj, the holy journey to Mecca, and often petitioned the Tsar for permission to travel. It was not until 1870, when Alexander recognized the desperation of the Imam's plea, that this permission was granted. Shamil had explained that he had had a premonition of his own death, nudging the Tsar's acquiescence.

Shamil, Allah's second prophet on earth, was not allowed to travel with his two eldest sons, though his wives and youngest children were permitted to accompany him. Their journey took them through Constantinople, south of the Caucasus, where, dismissing the Sultan's offers of grand palaces, the seventy-four-year-old Imam opted for a large, plain house that held its own mosque. Some months later, an ailing Shamil reached Mecca. The crowds gathered about him. Wherever he prayed, temples were crushed full of people. The mullahs were forced to allot him his own time to pray in private.

It was a strange journey, from the heights of the Dagestani mountains, through Chechen forests, to Russian suburbia and finally to Mecca. Throughout his life, Shamil had never deviated once from his faith, and so his passage from Mecca to Medina was particularly apt. Medina was called the City of the Prophet and housed the remains of Mohammed. To the Muslims it is considered only second in importance to Mecca, in the same way as Shamil was measured to Mohammed. The Imam's last written words were dispatched to Russia: 'My final request is that you will make it possible for all the members of my family to gather in one place after my death, lest they become like a flock of sheep without a shepherd.' Sent with this missive was the request that his sons might come to him. Permission was denied by the Tsar. Shamil died under the impression that his sons were soon to arrive, thoroughly convinced of the munificence of the Russian empire.

CHAPTER 23

# The Echoes of Blood

*Last week, before we left Georgia, we had arranged a final*
*interview. In the old part of Tbilisi, along narrow tree-lined*
*streets, is a small apartment building with a central staircase*
*that seems full of echoes. The sound of one man's footsteps is*
*like a regiment on the march. On the second floor lives a lady*
*called Tamara Shamil, the great-great-granddaughter of the*
*third Imam of Dagestan.*

In her fifties, Tamara is a very assured woman. She retains a
beauty, a grace and a strength that it is impossible to see as anything
other than a genetic echo passed down through history. We are
invited into her apartment, where we share wine, tea and an enormous cream cake that has been prepared in our honour. Family
photographs are drawn from dusty files, and the generations of her
family are laid before us, eyes rising from faded photographs, back
to the portrait of Shamil taken in Kaluga that had so delighted the
*naibs*.

There are books as well, though the Georgian script is impossible to decipher. She picks one up. 'This', she says, 'is a pro-Russian

book, written by the head of Shamil's security on the Russian side.' I cannot be sure, but it is most likely she is referring to Runovsky's account. 'It is deceitful, a piece of propaganda. It tells of how happy he was in captivity, how he liked everything Russian, that he adored the country, loved the Tsar. How can he have been so happy, when so many of his family died on Russian ground?'

Of course, the Imam's thoughts are lost to us. Was Runovsky trustworthy in his account? Did he see what he wished to see, ignorant of his captives' true feelings? We cannot know. It is true, however, that out of the thirty-four men and women, either direct members of Shamil's family or of his faithful *naibs*, exactly half died before the Imam. All were victims of forms of consumption, brought on by the change of climate. Such losses must have weighed heavily on Shamil. His decision not to die fighting the Russians was influenced by a need to protect his family. Still, even the Imam could not protect them from aching hearts, homesickness, guttural coughs and slow deaths.

It was as if the Russians had beaten not only Shamil but his entire people, his whole culture. He had been greeted as a piece of exotica, a fading representation that would never be imitated. He had been hunted, driven to ground and captured. The Lion of Dagestan was a zoological rarity. Caged in Kaluga, they had come to stare, for they would not see his like again. Veterans of the Caucasus had never been turned away from the house. Men who had lost friends, brothers, fathers to the Murids came to pay their respects, to talk of blood long since shed. Neither of the accounts of Shamil's captivity ever mentions the question of *why* they had fought being raised. It was as if, after the sounds of battle had faded, the memory of war was enough for the Russians. The war for the Caucasus had been fought, long and hard, for over thirty years. To keep talking of Caucasian battles and heroes was to build the myth, to bring a sweet cloud of romance down upon one of the bloodiest episodes in Russian history.

In Shamil's own family, a distinct legacy was passed on, though the mountains seem to have been extracted from the blood. The name Shamil, of course, still cuts a swathe through the people of the Caucasus. Tamara was raised in Georgia. During her college examinations she had prepared herself well for the strenuous oral test.

'What is your name?' she was asked by the professor.

'Tamara Shamil.'

'What? Shamil?' He opened the door and called in his fellows. 'Everybody come here.'

At every exam, the same thing happened. After a while, her girlfriends became annoyed. She admits she never really had to take an exam. 'You are riding on your name,' they accused her, 'the same way your grandmother rode in her carriage.'

Tamara shrugs at the memory and grins. 'It wasn't my fault. Perhaps it was bad for me.'


Her great-grandfather was Shamil's youngest son. He was born in Kaluga, the last son of Zaidette, and was orphaned at the age of twelve. With the Tsar's permission, he returned to Dagestan. His first born, named Jamal al-Din after his brother that he never knew, was sent to St Petersburg as a young man, to join the Cadet Corps. It was an honour usually reserved for the rich, noble or well connected. While still serving the Tsar, there was an insurrection in the Georgian province of Guria, and Jamal al-Din was chosen as one of the officers to lead the Russian punitive expedition.

'My grandmother', continues Tamara, 'was a Gurian princess. My grandfather Jamal al-Din, you see, was stationed at her house. Perhaps it was a paradox that Grandfather fought for the Russians, but it was so. My grandfather ignored my grandmother, but befriended her father. Every day, when he was stationed there, they would go hunting, play chess, sit and read together, feed the dogs. My grandmother would tell me that she would get mad. Here was this handsome young officer and he wouldn't even look at her. It continued this way for six months.

'One day he asked her father if he might take this princess out for a ride. Of course you must, I trust you. He helped her on her horse and rode off with her. He did not come back, he had kidnapped her.'

It was a moment of romantic drama, for Jamal al-Din was a curious hybrid. Enough of the mountaineer ran through his blood to consider such a ritual, yet he was to continue to serve the Tsar. His manner was far from uncouth. By all accounts, he was a man of great charm who managed to appeal to both his Muslim brethren and fellow officers. His treatment of his future wife was almost gallant, if the act of kidnapping is seen as a purely romantic gesture.

'He did not rape her,' says Tamara, 'he did not insult her in any way. He simply carried her to a house where he had hired women servants, then left her there. Ten days later he came back and told her that she was free to leave. Of course, she was not free to leave. Should she return to her father, it would be in disgrace. They would think she had been shamed. But my grandmother always said, "I liked him, all in all I liked him."'

There were, of course, problems. A Muslim son-in-law was deemed unacceptable and the two lived quietly together until Tamara's father was born in 1910. With a male child in hand, Jamal al-Din decided that it was time to introduce his bride to his family and returned to Dagestan. Tamara's grandmother remembered her mother-in-law as a 'beauty, tall and stately, with a hundred braids. When she entered a house, everyone would stand up and nobody dared to sit down until she had taken a seat.' Soon, though, the duty of soldiery called, and Jamal al-Din left his wife and child with his mother and returned to the lowlands. Fortunately for Tamara's grandmother, there were several Georgian soldiers stationed near by, one of whom informed the young wife that her mother-in-law wished her dead, so that the child might be raised as a Muslim. With a small company of Georgian soldiers, Tamara's grandmother fled through the night for the border. From there she rode alone, the child in one arm, a pistol tucked into her waistband.

'She would never return to Dagestan,' says Tamara. 'But with the child's religion at stake, she was welcomed back into her family, though she was forced to convert to Lutheranism, for they allow marriages between faiths. In 1914, the Great War began. My grandfather went to fight for the Russians, but after two years his letters stopped coming. No letters ever arrived again, his body was lost. My family remained in Georgia. My father became completely Georgian. I feel, well, I *am* Georgian.'

The push and pull that came to live within Shamil was passed on through the generations. Shamil's interest in both the Bible and the Koran continued among his descendants. The schisms created within his own life, and more notably within the two Jamal al-Dins continued into the twentieth century. They were devout Muslims, living between two stronger Christian states of Georgia and Russia. Mountaineers, surrounded by steppe lands. Family men, bred to be warriors. Members of a holy war who ended by swearing faith to the Tsar. They were lives lived between captors and captives. Only in Tamara's generation has the ebb and flow lessened. Perhaps blood, like water, flows down from the mountains, leaving behind the turbulence of rapids, finding an unexpected serenity in the plains.

# CHAPTER 24

# Into the Black Garden

*The road that lies between Yerevan and the mountainous region*

*of Karabagh is perhaps the best in all the Caucasus. The tar is*

*so smooth you feel that a marble released in Karabagh might*

*roll its way into the streets of Yerevan. As a result, it is the least*

*painful of all our drives. Ilya is reasonably quiet, trying to*

*control a small hangover. Somewhere he has found a wad of*

*plasticine and amuses himself by shaping it into a large phal-*

*lus and placing it on the dashboard.*

John is still bristling from the morning before. Ilya had refused to wake up from a deep sleep for a sunrise shoot, leaving John few options. The shouting, the shaking, the shoving did not work. A bucket of water over the head did. Ilya woke up, spitting curses, then reluctantly got dressed and stepped into the car, with one hour of sleep and many shots of vodka coursing through his veins. After shooting two red lights, John tried to attach his seat-belt made of string, but the clasp was gone.

'You're drunk,' John had said. 'Slow down.'

'Ilya drunk,' said Ilya. 'Ilya drunk again.'

Somewhere between the suburbs of Yerevan and the city, Ilya took a wrong turn. The sun was still not up, but he then decided it would be best if they evaded the police by driving without headlights. By the time they met Taran, John was stony faced and pale. Ilya spent the rest of the day asleep in the back seat.

Morning in Armenia is a remarkable time. There is no reason for it, no reason for the light to fall differently on this part of the Caucasus than anywhere else. I am reminded of our meeting two days ago with Vartan Oskanian, Armenia's Foreign Minister. 'Our country is different,' he had said. 'We are different, we should be different.' Under such strange light, it is hard to doubt his words. It is a light made of gold and silvers, a richness that can change all colours and textures it touches, can make marble out of cement, sculpt a red ocean out of a barren desert. Halfway to Karabagh, we are greeted by a rainbow that drapes from the sky in three separate arcs. I have never seen this before. Perhaps it is unique to Armenia.

Despite the good roads, it is a long day, interrupted by frustrating conversations.

'How far are we? Halfway?'

'No, we are more than halfway,' says Ilya.

'How far have we gone?'

'One hundred and eighty kilometres.'

'How far do we have to go?'

'One hundred and eighty kilometres.' Ilya shrugs.

'So we *are* halfway.'

'Yes, I tell you, we are halfway.'

Karabagh, a Persian word for 'Black Garden', was the first battleground in the wake of the downfall of communism. Countries granted a sudden independence looked about one another, like men unhooded in bright sunlight. Armenia, Georgia and Azerbaijan, the three countries of the Transcaucasus, had to make immediate decisions. While Armenia decided to bind itself to Russia, allowing military bases to remain as open displays of muted Russian influence, Georgia was swept into a brief and bloody internal conflict, Russia exerting considerable pressure to keep her former state close to her side. Azerbaijan took an even more risky path. Sometimes known as the 'cork' to the 'bottle' of the Caspian, Azerbaijan was in a powerful economic position to flirt with the West. Turkey, America, France and Britain were quick to respond to her potential oil wealth. It was now not just a religious schism in the Transcaucasus but a prospective economic one as well. In a way, it helped to isolate Azerbaijan, even from her Muslim neighbours. Iran, which borders to the south, contains twenty million native Azeris and is wary that an economically successful Azerbaijan might fracture her own state. Relations between the countries remain cool, despite the bonds of Shiite Islam.

In 1990, when Armenia launched an offensive to seize approximately 20 per cent of Azerbaijan's territory, in the region of Karabagh, there was no concerted reaction. Armenia, so long the international victim, had recognized the weakness of the Azeri position. Azerbaijan, without outside military help, was a poorly defended enemy, divided by bickering politicians. In Karabagh, both the Armenian and Azerbaijani citizens suffered. It was a war not driven by religion but by the ugliness of ethnic cleansing. Many were killed, the rest driven deeper into their homelands.

Whose land was Karabagh? This is the question, argued from both sides by a plethora of politicians, historians and anthropologists, that lies at the heart of the Karabagh issue. It is, undoubtedly, a land populated by Christian churches, but for every ecclesiastic fact that supports the claim of Armenia, a corresponding claim can be made for Azerbaijan. Since the eleventh century,

Karabagh had always been a part of one empire or another: first Georgian, then Mongol, Turkish, Persian, Russian and finally Soviet. It was only when the powers of the region receded that the question of autonomy could even be raised. For Azerbaijan, it was enough that the Russians had always tried to tie Karabagh to Baku. For 170 years it had been so. The Armenian memory runs deeper, the pages turned back to before the division of their kingdom in 387 BC.

The Armenians maintain that their intent was clear: they wished to reclaim what they saw as their historical legacy. Though, at one time, there was enough advantage and momentum that they might have pushed much deeper into Azerbaijani territory, they halted their advance in 1992 near the borders of Karabagh. While, for Armenia and Azerbaijan, Karabagh was a territorial but never a religious war, this did not stop others from viewing the conflict as Muslim versus Christian. Men from the north Caucasus descended from the mountains to side with the Azerbaijanis. In their quest for a pan-Islamic Caucasus, a certain group headed south from Chechnya. At their head was a twenty-eight-year-old veteran of the Soviet army, committed to vague ideals of freedom, independence and Allah. He was called Shamil Basayev, named after the Imam who had been dead now for over a hundred years.

As early as November 1991 Basayev had laid claim to ignominy when he had hijacked an Aeroflot plane with 178 passengers. Chechnya had just announced its independence and the Russian President, Boris Yeltsin, had responded by suspending constitutional rights and dispatching troops to Grozny. The aeroplane was forced to fly first to Ankara, then to Grozny, where all the hostages were released unharmed. Russia branded this a terrorist act, while the Turkish Government labelled it an 'act of protest' in which

Basayev sought to direct the world's attention to his then-unknown state of Chechnya. Yeltsin opted to back down; the troops he had sent to Grozny were withdrawn on buses. It was the slightest taste of what was to come.

Basayev seemed to appear wherever his Muslim brothers were rising. In Abkhazia, he was to lead a small force of Chechens against Christian Georgia. It was the custom of his unit to howl like wolves before attacking, then shout, 'The Chechens are coming, the Chechens are coming.' 'When we'd get to the top of a hill,' said Basayev, 'there was never anyone there.' In Chechnya, there is an expression, 'To be as free as a wolf,' a little more threatening than our avian equivalent. It was the same tactic that the Chechens had used against the Russians in the Murid campaigns and had a sharp psychological effect that often terrified raw recruits more than gunfire.

Knowing of his magnetic attraction to warfare, it was unsurprising to find Shamil Basayev beside his Azerbaijani brethren in Karabagh, attempting to repel the Armenian assault near the town of Shusha. Of all the towns located in the disputed region, no loss was more deeply felt for the Azeris than that of Shusha. Its name means glass, derived from a vast conservatory built by Panakh Khan in the seventeenth century. It was an oasis intended for writers and artists. As the Persian army approached, a warning was issued: 'God is pouring stones upon your head. Sit ye not then in thy fortress of glass.' Despite the threats, Shusha was never taken but the ironic title of City of Glass remained.

By 1992, the fragility of glass was an all too accurate metaphor. Perhaps such an ancient aura of invincibility led the Azeris to defend it so poorly. As a result, it was taken in a two-day battle. One of the veterans, sitting next to his wooden leg beside a ruined building tells me, 'The Azeris ran. What can I say? We were coming and they ran.' The mosque in Shusha lies at the end of a bombed-out street. It is pocked by artillery, gutted by fire. Inside it is littered with a dirty mixture of weeds and trash. You can look into apartment buildings and tell exactly which were the homes of Azeri or Armenian.

As Shamil Basayev now found out, his Muslim brothers in Azerbaijan were hardly mountain warriors bred in the Imam's shadow. Whatever Shamil Basayev was expecting, he cannot have been enthused by the discipline and commitment of his Muslim allies. An Azeri war reporter put it bluntly. 'I saw Basayev in Shusha. He was disgusted. He came here to fight, but he finds that Azerbaijani do not make good soldiers. We trade well, but fighting, no, it is not good for us. But there is one thing, very important, that Basayev takes from Karabagh. This was his training ground. Without Karabagh, he would not fight the Russians so well in Chechnya.'

# CHAPTER 25

# The Shadow of Shamil

*One hundred and thirty-five years after the surrender of Imam*

*Shamil at Gounib, his ghost would rise again. In 1994, Russia*

*stumbled blindly into the Chechen conflict. The presumption was*

*that the Chechens had as much taste for war as many of the*

*other troubled spots across the former Soviet Union. The appear-*

*ance of soldiers and tanks was usually more than enough to*

*extinguish the sparks of rebellion. In the case of Chechnya,*

*though, the Russian High Command had not been reading its*

*history.*

The first attempt to stabilize Grozny was a humiliating disaster. The Russian Defence Minister, General Grachev, was later to admit that the entire planning of the invasion began only one month before the first tank rolled across the border. The day before Russia entered Chechnya, Grachev had reputedly boasted that a single airborne regiment could capture Grozny in two hours. It was a twentieth-century echo of the past, concentrated and delivered in ignorance.

Even more true in 1994 than it had been in the nineteenth century was the fact that Russian character was derived from its relation to the state. Only now, it was a state in decline, and the morale of the military was even lower than Russian commanders suspected. The Associated Press reported that in the first weeks of the war, unpaid Russian soldiers began selling their ammunition and weapons to local Chechens. In early 1995 there was a confirmed report that an armoured personnel carrier had changed hands for several thousand American dollars.

Contrarily, the Chechens had kept alive many of their customs, in a country that still drew heavily from its ethnic tradition. Many Russians could not place Chechnya on a map, yet the Chechens had forgotten nothing about Russia. There in Grozny stood the statue of General Yermolov to remind them. Busts of Stalin were particularly despised. In 1944, towards the end of the Second World War, Stalin had taken the decision to deport the entire Chechen population. He accused them, *en masse*, of collaborating with the Germans, even those who had been fighting for Russia in the steppe lands. A nation was herded together within days, driven from the mountains, gathered in the plains, then forced towards the stations and waiting trains.

Until Khrushchev reversed the decision in 1957, the Chechen people were in exile, some as far as Siberia, most in the deserts of Kazakhstan. The railways that had carried the population south from Grozny in 1944 were little better than steel lines of death. During the thousand-mile journey one-quarter of all Chechens perished. The surviving exiles were those who had nurtured the generation maturing in the 1990s. Though many Russians moved into Chechnya by Stalin continued to live in Chechen cities, they were rarely welcome in the mountains. Even so, it was the Russian state that was despised, rather than her people.

As the journalist and historian Anatol Lieven reports, 'Russian soldiers will fight hard to defend their country if it is attacked . . . they just need to be told why they are fighting, and to be sure that they are being told the truth.' When the tanks pulled into Grozny in 1994, they had little to no idea of what their purpose was. Lieven reported that a nineteen-year-old driver of an armoured personnel carrier conceded, 'We had no map . . . the commander ran for it. We were lost, the Chechens were all around us and firing . . . I did not want to be their enemy, to come here and kill other farmers. I am a farmer myself. If Yeltsin wants this war, let him come and fight himself.'[17]

The Chechens were fighting in small groups. As in the nineteenth century, from an early age, they were familiar with weapons. Most groups numbered twenty or less, all from the same village. Normally a man with some military knowledge was chosen as a 'sergeant', and since many of the older Chechens had served in the Soviet army there was no shortage of experience. As one local at the time put it, 'This is not an army. It is the whole Chechen people which is fighting.' Martin Van Creveld, in his book *The Transformation of War*, explains, 'It is worth pointing out that tribal societies, which do not have the state, also do not recognize the distinction between army and people. Such societies do not have armies; it would be more accurate to say that they themselves are armies.'[18]

Recruitment in Chechnya, throughout the war, continued to operate village by village, family by family. Russia, as a state rooted in Christianity, had come to believe in the separation between men of the Church and men of war. For the Muslims there was no such conflict. Mohammed was a warrior, Shamil, the Imam of Dagestan, had been a warrior. It is a right, stated within the Koran, that a man might rise armed against the infidels.

Young Russian soldiers were given little training, were ill-informed, underfed and sent into combat against a population determined to win independence. At first the reporters covering the conflict were sceptical about the Chechen likelihood of success. All across the world, they had witnessed men shooting their weapons into the air and boasting that they would repel superior forces, only to see them melt at the first onset of artillery fire. After all, only three years before, Russia was a superpower. In Grozny, the myth would unravel.

In the neighbourhoods of Grozny that the Russians managed to hold, they made no friends. Reports of looting, of civilian casualties, of rape and murder were common. It was foolhardy of the Russians. Chechnya in 1994 was a country that remembered its sufferings, and far from all of her people were anxious to engage the Russian forces. Only after war crimes against civilians spread did support for the rebels gather until all were rooted in a cohesive hatred of Russia. In the nineteenth century, Shamil had proved, alongside his Chechen allies, to be a master tactician, a man who employed nature against the enemy. The Russians were to find that the concrete jungle of Grozny was similarly impenetrable and just as threatening as the Argoun Forest. Every building shattered by artillery fire became a sniper's paradise.

If the Russians and the Chechens emerged from two very different societies, then their concepts of war and battlefield also remained in opposition. Few lessons were learned from the Russian military who had fought 150 years before, nor from more ancient military blunders. The Persian Darius once cleared eight square miles of fields by the Tigris for the use of his chariots. As with the Chinese before him, Darius believed that a battlefield should be prepared, that Alexander the Great would meet him head on, on selected and even ground. Instead, Alexander waited for four days, studying the Persian battle plan that lay so clearly before him, and finally drove Darius quickly from the field. The Chechens, unfortunately for the Russians, were as unconcerned with open fields of battle as were their fore-fathers. They knew they must turn their ground, the city streets of Grozny, to their advantage. In scenes reminiscent of the splintered columns of 1845's Biscuit Expedition, tanks and armoured cars were cut off from one another. Many had been supplied with broken radios. They were either captured or destroyed. With the Russians choosing to launch their attack in December, the invading military was often faced with thick fog, low clouds and rain. Even the versa-tile tank is vulnerable in thick mud and mountains, even the aero-plane cannot fly in poor weather.

The names of the rivers, the towns, the mountains where the conflict unravelled are already familiar to us: the Terek, Dargo, the Argoun Valley. Men were standing on the same ground that their great-grandfathers had stood on before them, in similar postures, weapons raised against the same foe. The losses incurred by Russia in the early summer of 1995 in Grozny were not replicated in the mountains. Near Dargo and Shatoi, the Chechens discovered that they had little more experience than the Russians in mountain warfare. Many of the beech forests were gone for ever, and such open ground proved indefensible. However, as in the nineteenth century, any success in combat against a greater force was inter-preted as reason enough to fight on.

In Baku, we had met with a Chechen who wished to show us a videotape that he claimed he had taken himself. It is hard to know who controlled the camera, but the footage is famous around the Caucasus. In 1995 a Russian armoured column moving up a narrow mountain road was hit in the van by a rocket-propelled grenade. All the tanks and armoured personnel carriers behind it were unable to pass. The grenades were being propelled from too steep an angle for the Russian tanks to return fire. The next tank to explode was the last in the column, trapping every vehicle in between. Twelve Chechens systematically destroyed every tank in the column.

Despite many successes, the Chechens were suffering heavily. Bombing runs by planes over Grozny had reduced all buildings of consequence to exposed ribcages, surrounded by moats of mud. Those who could leave the city did, often fleeing towards the mountains. Grozny, after all, had only been built as a Russian fort in 1818, and only attracted a large Chechen population after the return from exile in 1957. Almost all of Grozny's Chechens had relatives who still lived in their original ancestral villages, and in a time of crisis, they were welcome there. It was, then, the Russian civilians who had nowhere to turn. Their own troops looted their houses, their own planes bombed their streets. Between 1994 and 1996, forty-five thousand people died in Chechnya. Of these, it is estimated that only three thousand were soldiers. The majority were Russian citizens of Grozny.

Fuelled by governmental criticism, the Russian military began to make headway on the other battlefields of Chechnya. The Russian media had gone from strict Soviet accountability in war zones to a sudden unparalleled access. Subsequently Russian television carried depressing live footage every night, often contradicting the military press releases of the day. It was a harrowing sight for a nation generally unsure why the war had started in the first place. Living rooms were lit by flickering images of teenage Russian soldiers being placed in coffins. Nevertheless, by January 1995, Grozny was surrounded on three sides, all airstrips in the vicinity controlled by the Russians.

The first attempt to take the city was as disastrous as the initial campaign. The Russian front, which was supposed to attack simultaneously from three different directions, barely moved at all, only one of the three columns reaching its intended destination. As a result, the Chechens were allowed to mass their forces against a third of the Russian troops 'Contact was lost with our forward units,' explained one general. Few escaped, many died, the rest became prisoners of war.

Often, the Chechens took pity on the youngest conscripts. It was easy to recognize that they were underfed, desperate to leave Chechnya, pitifully undertrained. However, as kindly as the conscripts were treated, mercenaries, known as *kontraktniks*, were subjected to harrowing ordeals. In Azerbaijan, we met with a Chechen who described their treatment of one such mercenary: 'He was paid one hundred and eighty dollars to fight Chechens. We capture him, big man, and inside his pockets we find a letter to his girlfriend. He has photograph inside too, of him in uniform. Smiling, looking brave and he is talking all the time of how he is killing Chechens. All lies, but he is talking. We make him naked, then he is dressed up in women's clothing and we put lipstick on him. Then we take photograph and put it in letter instead and send letter to his girlfriend. Then we cut his throat.'

By early February, after several false starts, the Russians made the Chechen position in the city so untenable, threatening the only Chechen-controlled road out of the city, that they were forced to abandon Grozny. Any overtures of peace were muddied by politicking on both sides. Internal pressures had already made Yeltsin and Grachev's relationship, as well as their positions, tenuous. They claimed that the two Chechen commanders, Dudayev and Maskhadov, had no centralized control, particularly of the man they had long ago labelled a terrorist, Shamil Basayev. While Basayev was still at large, claimed the Russians, there would be no peace talks.

Grozny, after such intense street-to-street fighting, was a city in ruins, all infrastructure destroyed. Success in the lowlands and mountains proved much more easy for the Russians. They pushed on towards the last two Chechen strongholds, Shatoi and Vedeno. The latter was not only where Shamil had made his longest stand in the Murid Wars, but was also the birthplace of Shamil Basayev. Knowing this, the Russians had launched a bombing raid on the town, presuming that by using a vacuum bomb, they were unlikely to miss the Chechen commander. Vacuum bombs are extremely effective, even reaching those hiding in bunkers. Victims die not from shrapnel, but from collapsed lungs, and are always found with bleeding noses. Though he was absent, eleven members of his family, all women and children, were killed. Lieven reports that at this time, 'Chechen fortunes were at . . . their lowest ebb of the entire war.'[19] He goes on to say that there was little ammunition left, the men were exhausted and morale was beginning to fray. These facts, combined with Shamil Basayev's personal motives, inspired his next move. It is not an act that should be glorified, though Basayev would emerge from what the *New York Times* was to call 'the greatest hostage strike of the century' as a hero to the Chechens.

# CHAPTER 26

# The History of Hostages

*There is nothing new in the Caucasus about the taking of hostages. Tamara Shamil's story of the kidnapping of her grandmother by her grandfather is familiar in Caucasian history. The kidnapping of a bride was not considered a crime but a ritual, both families often content when the young rider would gallop up to his intended, throw her over the saddle and disappear. Today, the echo still rings through Georgia. Gela Charkviani, adviser to President Eduard Shevardnadze, reminisced how his son kidnapped his bride: 'He took her from the street, put her in his car and drove away. It is like elopement, but being kidnapped is more romantic.' Another theory is that with such a stress on manhood in the Caucasus, few men concentrate on education. Women of the same age are allowed to do little other than educate themselves. Unable to impress their erudite fiancées, the youths resort to kidnapping.*

George Sava, the Georgian author, had the process explained to him by his guardian, a mountaineer called Shota, at the beginning of the twentieth century. First, clarified the older man, the love between the two young people was established through glances. Then, when the young man is certain of his love, he dispatches a delegation of his relatives to hand over 'her price . . . a present for having reared such a beautiful daughter'.

And if, asked Sava, he comes from a poor family?

'He goes out and makes money . . . probably on a thieving expedition.'

'Supposing he can't find a fat merchant, what then?' Sava had finally understood that wife-stealing and raids were both economic issues.

'If his love is strong, he merely kidnaps the girl. He creeps up to the house at night, or perhaps when the maiden is unprotected for a moment, and swings her on to his saddle and away they go.'

Fathers with only daughters stood to lose heavily on the financial transaction, yet once a girl was kidnapped there was great shame in taking her back within the house. In the end, the ritual seems directed to favour the bold, certainly not to favour the intended bride. In a tradition of thievery and warriors, it ultimately seems like a dry run for the more common economic activity – kidnapping from the plains.

In 1858, Alexandre Dumas, at the height of his fame, wrote an account of his journey through the Caucasus. He commented that 'seldom does a night pass without someone being carried off for ransom'. This should be taken with a considerable pinch of salt. The writer of *The Man in the Iron Mask* also wrote, when confused how the Imam Shamil had escaped from a mountaintop, that 'perhaps some eagle had wafted him away through the clouds' or that 'gnomes had led him through the bowels of the earth to safety'.

Dumas sought to amuse with his exaggerations, but his fictions were based on fact.

Hostage-taking was simply an extension of the traditional raid. When the men galloped into the plains, it was not merely goods and livestock that they were after, but also human captives. Some were used as slaves to till the land, but most were returned to relatives for ransom. Since the end of the war in Chechnya in 1996, the destroyed economy has left hostage-taking the most lucrative available business.

Mamuka Areshidze is the Georgian Government's Expert on Relations with the North Caucasus. He has a stout body and the head of a bull, with eyes that do nothing short of glare. During his tenure, he has negotiated the release of twelve Georgians. He states that there were still twenty-six Georgians being held captive in Chechnya, all in a small town not far across the border. There are also many Chechens kept there, he adds. Earlier in our journey, Ali Asaev, the unofficial Chechen Ambassador to Azerbaijan, had promised us that the habit of Chechens kidnapping one another had now died out. Areshidze smiles. 'He lied to you.'

All of the hostage negotiations conducted by Areshidze have been concluded in northern Georgia, along the border with Chechnya at a village called Shateli that he says is safe enough for us to visit. Ordinarily, it would have seemed an extreme diversion to head for Shateli, being only two hundred miles from our final destination of Baku. However, the borders of Karabagh and Azerbaijan remain mined and are still defended by a standing army of approximately sixteen thousand men. The only way to pass from Karabagh to Azerbaijan is to head back into Armenia, then through Georgia, leaving us the option of heading north for Shateli.

The village itself is set against a dramatic backdrop, stone houses rising from a river bed, steep hills on either side. George Sava, writing at the turn of the last century, described it as 'luxurious country, fertile, heavily wooded with oak trees, which grew to an enormous size, and sometimes stood so close together that they resembled a gigantic barricade'. There were few such huge trees left when we arrive, and the village is virtually deserted.

Shateli has become a symbol of ambiguity, poised on the river banks between Christian and Muslim nations, silent as a museum at sunrise, halfway between Grozny and Tbilisi. It is an eerie monument. The Soviets emptied the village by force eighty years ago, leaving it to the snows. Only five families live among the stones now, all engaged in rebuilding the *aoul*, house by house, having returned soon after the collapse of the Soviet Union. In the intervening years, Shateli stood alone, a ghost town with steep stone paths separated by tufts of coarse grass. It is a marker, the evidence that even an empty *aoul* can survive desolate winters and outlast yet another empire. Some houses have no roofs, some no beams, some seem exhausted, their stones poised to spill inwards and founder. It is a sombre place, even on such a beautiful morning. Perhaps it had become accustomed to being forgotten and resents its restoration, resents the fickleness of man.

Taran and I walk through it, alone at sunrise. Two days before I had lost my temper, screamed at Taran for a half-hour over the topic of the front seat of the car. He had looked at me in absolute mystification, not knowing why such a petty thing had led me to boiling point. I had become convinced that I was being slighted, and, worst of all, I was sure I was being slighted subconsciously. A subconscious slight, I had reasoned, is far worse than a deliberate slight because it showed a natural reaction. I couldn't stop the vitriolic words that spilled out against my oldest friend as I had struggled to explain my thoughts. He had just sat on the ground like Buddha and waited for the storm to pass.

'It's Ilya, isn't it?' he had whispered. 'He's finally gotten to you.'

Our Uzbek translator was the only one who had enjoyed the showdown. During my rant, especially when I had begged Taran to stand so that we could fight for the front seat, Ilya kept up a steady chant of 'Kill him, kill him, kill him.' John just stood by the side of the road and shook his head, considering my performance a variation of cabin fever.

In Shateli, Taran and I talk again. I try to sweep pettiness from my mind, but the daily routine is insidious. I am finding this grudge hard to dispel. Still, the morning turns out to be one of the most peaceful moments of the journey, most likely because I can see Ilya asleep by the river beneath us. An old woman herding cows passes him and veers up a mountain track. Out of one of the stone doorways the soles of a pair of feet seem to be suspended in mid-air. I peer, then squint. It is a mule, his white ears wagging back and forth as he shakes his head.

There are carvings above each door, human hands etched into the stones. They signify the number of lives claimed in any one vendetta. To prove that you had killed a man, you had to return with his right hand. There are so many scattered through the houses that I find myself holding my right wrist in my left hand. It feels exposed.

A mile outside Shateli, lying beside the river, is the carcass of a downed helicopter. Taran and I walk past Ilya, still asleep, then past John, nestled on the far bank. He has carried a fishing rod across the mountains and is now casting his fly again and again, content in his private world. A small stone hut, protection for a lonely pair of Georgian border guards, sits on the other side of the river. It looks bleak enough in the summer, but must be the most unenviable of positions when the snows lie deep. The likelihood of seeing, let alone stopping, cross-border activity at Shateli is small. The only communications between Georgia and Chechnya, one imagines, are deliberate and pre-planned.

The Murid Wars were marked by hostage strikes: the abduction of Jamal al-Din by the Russians and the capture of the Georgian princesses being the most notable examples. Neither they nor the Shateli negotiations, however, can be compared to the boldness or the tactical importance of the strike led by Shamil Basayev in May 1995.

# CHAPTER 27

# The Resurrection of Shamil

*Driving two trucks and a hand-painted 'police vehicle', Basayev*
*crossed the border into Russia. He travelled with 150 chosen*
*fighters and 25,000 American dollars. There are differing reports*
*on how he got so deep into enemy territory. A Russian jour-*
*nalist, familiar with the land, said that the guarded roads were*
*for the 'stupid, the law-abiding and the wealthy who did not*
*mind being fleeced by the patrols. For the rest there is the Mother*
*Steppe with its myriad dirt tracks.' Basayev himself was asked*
*how he managed to drive past army and police checkpoints. The*
*Chechens, he answered, had dressed as Russian mercenaries,*
*pretending that the trucks were loaded with dead bodies. Every*
*checkpoint suspected that the trucks really carried looted goods*
*from Grozny. They did not check the backs of the trucks, but*
*demanded bribes. How much? 'From one hundred for the entire*
*post, to five thousand dollars . . .' And why had he stopped at*

*Budennovsk? Simply because he had run out of money to grease the palms of the police.*

Budennovsk is 120 kilometres north of the Chechen border, a large, unattractive town with a population of 100,000 rising from an expanse of wheatfields. Just outside Budennovsk a roadblock refused him passage, Basayev claiming to have only a hundred dollars left on him. The convoy turned around and drove into the town centre. A police car led him to the militia headquarters, unsuspecting of Basayev's cargo. Adjacent to the headquarters was a large hospital. As the trucks pulled up, a gun battle erupted. Their police escorts were shot at close range, and several Chechens were killed, others wounded. Basayev's original intention was to fight from the local town hall, but with his own wounded to care for he opted for the hospital. 'Emergency doctors', he later explained, 'happen to be men of honour.' A running gun battle was conducted in the mile from the town hall to the hospital. Every house that was fought through was emptied of its occupants, who were herded beside the gunmen, callously employed as human shields. By the time they reached the hospital thirty-five people had died, including eight Chechens.

Two thousand patients were sealed into the hospital with Basayev's men. They were to spend the next eight days together. Realizing that they were dealing with a large, well-armed group, the local authorities alerted the army. A perimeter was set up and Budennovsk was encircled by rings of troops, politicians and, most importantly, the media. Demands were issued. Basayev stated the condition for hostage release: the cessation of combat in Chechnya, the withdrawal of Russian troops and the entry of both sides into negotiations. He announced that he would like to meet with journalists. Thirty reporters volunteered to enter the grounds of the hospital to attend this strange briefing. The Russian authorities were hesitant to bow to such a concession. They were forced to watch the execution of five Russian pilots in the gardens of the hospital before they granted permission for the reporters to proceed.

A journalist from *Izvestiya* described their progress inside the walls.

We walked up to the second floor of the hospital which was full of hostages, crouching or sitting on the floor. Our passage was interrupted by a sudden and furious exchange of fire. More windows were broken, there was loud crying in the halls. We were lying on the floor together, with these terror-ists cursing at the Russians who had promised not to shoot.

The Russian decision to fire at the gathering of Russian journal-ists is unexplained. One of the reporters inside later questioned a member of the Russian federal staff: 'Did you know that the room that was intended for the press conference was fired on?'

'Yes, I did,' replied the officer. 'But our troops were not aware there was any conference at all.'

At the conference, a bearded and calm Basayev repeated his demands, stressing that Russia must cease the war in Chechnya, and that negotiations must begin between President Yeltsin, Prime Minister Chernomyrdin and the Chechen President, Dudayev.

'We are tired of watching how our women, old people, kids are murdered,' said Basayev. 'We are tired of watching our villages get bombed . . . so we have come to Russian villages. We do not intend to kill any of the hostages. We will not shoot women and children, we are not maniacs. The worst that can happen is that the Russian army will murder them if they choose to storm the building.'

'What about your own death?' asked a reporter.

'Man is mortal.' Basayev shrugged. 'We do not care when we die. Only how we die.'

It was, in many ways, a similar strike to the centuries-old *nabeg*, the sudden raid from mountain to plain. However, Basayev's aim was not economic, but political. Even Shamil's raid on Tsinondali turned out to have financial motives. His *naibs* were as equally insistent on the financial reward of forty thousand silver roubles as they were for the return of Jamal al-Din. If Basayev's aim was purer, his manner was much bloodier. He knew that the more blood spilled in Russia, the more international focus would be drawn on Chechnya. He knew full well such a raid might turn international opinion against him, but there had been no benefits from international sympathy. In addition, any breathing room that he could buy the Chechen fighters would be priceless, regardless of his own fate.

Special forces units were deployed about the hospital. Basayev, ever watchful, pushed hostages into each window and declared that should an attempt be made to storm the building, they would die. Three days after the hospital was taken, with President Yeltsin absent in Canada attempting to secure loans at a G7 meeting, Russian special forces attacked at dawn: 'We could no longer delay the assault because of the actual threat to hostages' lives.' NTV, among other news channels, taped every minute of the assault. Grenade launchers destroyed five Russian armoured personnel carriers as the special forces converged on the hospital from all angles.

It was a scene of chaos inside the hospital, the Russian forces entering the ground floor, grenades bursting all about, hostages huddled in corners under mattresses. The Chechens thrust hostages through second-floor windows. Some were killed immediately by Russian snipers, but the cries of the others, their pleas for a ceasefire, were heard and all shooting stopped. One hundred and twenty-one civilians had either died or been wounded in the rescue attempt. Reported Russian military casualties were suspiciously low. On the second floor of the hospital, the remaining Chechens were still in control of around one thousand hostages.

Amazingly, despite the fact that the first assault resulted in as many deaths as hostages rescued, the special forces attacked the hospital for a second time later that day. It was not nearly as consolidated an effort as its bloody precursor and was easily repulsed by the Chechens. Contrary to the 'actual threat to their lives' the rescued women reported that the terrorists had been treating them well, sharing their food and obtaining chocolate for their children.

There were a handful of casualties shared evenly between the Chechens and the attacking unit, yet over a hundred hostages had died. All was captured on film by the Russian media and shared throughout the nation. Shortly after the second raid, Basayev released another 150 hostages, the majority women and children. The original order for the storming of the building had come not from a commander on the ground, with a firm understanding of the situation, but directly from Yeltsin, sitting in Halifax, Nova Scotia.

Two more days dragged on before the Russians agreed to negotiate with Basayev. Despite the act of pure aggression against civilians, it was already a publicity coup in favour of Chechnya. Originally dismissed as a 'dirty, bearded terrorist', Basayev was now conducting a live interview with the Prime Minister of Russia. Chernomyrdin was ready to capitulate. The transcript shows how untenable the Russian position had become.

Chernomyrdin asks, 'Is this enough? Now release the women and children . . . listen, I beg you, I beg you, release the women and children, don't do that again, no more . . . I beg you.'

Chernomyrdin met with Basayev four times, finally consenting to all demands, though both agreed that the ceasefire in Chechnya would be temporary. Another four hundred hostages were released in good faith.

Basayev was to return to Chechnya with 'professional' hostages, mostly journalists who volunteered to accompany the remaining Chechens to the border. The two trucks wound their way south, accompanied by a refrigerated lorry that held the fourteen Chechen dead.

The talks began, and a ceasefire was signed on 21 June.

In Budennovsk, the doctors and nurses who had survived the eight-day captivity sat in the main square and began to denounce the way that the Russians had handled the situation, blaming their decision to storm the hospital for the majority of the 142 civilian deaths. Two hundred more had been wounded.

For the Chechens to have emerged from the situation with any honour at all seemed remarkable. What the Russians saw as a callous terrorist act was, in Chechnya, seen as a political statement, albeit merciless. Somehow Russia had bungled the whole situation: finally they had the proof that the Chechens were terrorists, just as the Russian Government had always said. So how had they then lost this bloody war of publicity? The nation had watched a terrible demonstration of inexperienced soldiery, brutal methods and total disregard for life. In many ways, the events of Budennovsk had been ample evidence for Chechen claims: the Russians were subject to a confused chain of command, iron-fistedness, a state displaying utter inhumanity. All this, despite the fact that the slaughter was brought about by Chechen action. Yeltsin survived the embarrassment, co-opting Chernomyrdin's success as peacemaker. However, public opinion polls in Russia showed anger equally aimed at Chechnya and Yeltsin's Government. With a new understanding of the war, the Russian people were given a stunning peek into the Russian incompetence and indiscriminate blood-letting that had, for so long, been typical of the conflict.

The wording of the ceasefire agreement contained no reference to Chechen independence. The Russians were aware of how close they had been to winning the war prior to the events in Budennovsk. They were unwilling to compromise after such effort and resources had been expended. Even so, Russia continued to be humiliated in the theatrics of television. To show that Chechens were beginning to disarm in their eagerness for peace, the Russian Government offered to pay roughly two hundred American dollars for weapons. Old men showed up with hunting guns, unused relics, broken rifles. The Chechens would collect their money, find a regiment of unpaid Russian soldiers, and buy their new AK-47s at discount prices. Arms and ammunition were gathered once again within the Chechen borders and a people on the edge of defeat had new reason for optimism.

Russian forces, deep in the mountains, were withdrawn after Budennovsk for tactical reconsideration, allowing the mass of Chechen fighters to slip, group by group, back into the plains. A summary given by the defence editor of *Segodnya* is a familiar echo of the reports of Russian lines during the war against Imam Shamil. 'In the lowlands, major Chechen units are exposed [but] advancing further would be quite difficult, supply lines becoming increasingly hard to manage. Vindicated by fighting around Vedeno, [the Chechens] might be able to begin a guerrilla campaign.'

The Russian answer was to rely more heavily than ever on aerial support. Entire villages suspected of cooperation were levelled using vacuum bombs. In April 1996, the Chechen President, Dudayev, used his satellite phone outside a mountain village. The coordinates were relayed from a passing Russian plane and seconds later a rocket erupted yards from him. Dudayev died immediately. By May, political pressures in Moscow demanded a cessation in the Chechen war. Yeltsin was desperate for re-election and had the backing of the Western world, despite repeated reports of human-rights violations in Chechnya. The rebel terrorists were welcomed inside the Kremlin, supposedly for a series of peace talks, politician to politician. The next day, Yeltsin declared that the war had been won, forgetting to inform his Chechen guests. All discussions with the rebels had been nothing but a pre-election gambit for votes. Bombing resumed in early July.

August saw the Russian offensive overwhelmed by a massive rebel attack on Grozny, led, once again, by Shamil Basayev. Fifteen hundred troops converged on the captured city, attacked predetermined posts, dissecting the city into zones of control. 'The actions in Grozny', said the new Chechen President, Aslan Mashkadov, in an interview with a Russian radio station, 'is to show that the war in Chechnya is not over yet.' In other words, the Kremlin had been revealed, once more, as a nest of incompetence and outright lies. It was a foggy morning and as refugees streamed from the city, the second wave of Chechen fighters entered, increasing the force to just over three thousand. These were not professional soldiers, but men dressed in jeans and sneakers, carrying Kalashnikovs and knives.

Early in the second day of the attack, a grenade hit the Russian ammunition store within the central government building of Grozny. The building was engulfed by fire. Every Russian column that was sent into the city to relieve the besieged outposts was ambushed and driven back. It was the very same mistake they had made when they had first attacked Grozny, the same mistakes that Vorontsov had made during the Biscuit Expedition 150 years before. Basayev announced to the press after the fourth day that

Grozny was back in Chechen hands. 'The Russians could take the city back,' he added, nursing a wound in his foot. 'They could take it in a month, but it would cost them ten to fifteen thousand men.'

General Lebed, who had led a Russian parachute regiment in Afghanistan, was handed the potentially disastrous role of closing this bloody chapter of Russian history. Granted full control of Russian forces by Yeltsin, he met with Mashkadov. They agreed that Russia could raze Chechnya, if it wished, but that it would be a costly victory. Lebed grasped the fact that the conflict had transformed a reasonably peaceful nation into a country of widows and children sympathetic to the concept of revenge. A fragile peace emerged from the early meetings. For the first time in the war, the ceasefire was respected by both sides. Perhaps it was a war that nobody had won, but in the eyes of the world, Russia had lost. Her troops were withdrawn from Grozny on 31 August.

The peace treaty that was signed made no mention of the status of Chechnya's independence. It would be deferred for five years. Fifty thousand civilians, approximately six thousand Russian troops and over three thousand Chechen fighters had died. 'All wars,' declared Lebed, 'even if they are hundred-year wars, end in negotiations and peace.'

# CHAPTER 28

# A Time to Leave

*From Shateli, we head south for Azerbaijan, passing one final night in Georgia's capital of Tbilisi on the way. To our delight, Mr Ramiz has kept his word and awaits us in Lado's house. All, however, is not well. Some time during our stay in Armenia, Lado's cousin, recently diagnosed with cancer, had died. She was not one of the eighteen living in our cosseted community, but knowing how close the bonds are in Lado's family, it is unsurprising that the sombre faces that greet us are etched in pain. That evening, amid long, sad toasts to the dead, the question of money is brought up. First, we are asked if we could help with funeral expenses, then once more if we could help with visas, and, finally, if we could defray money owed to us for refitting the borrowed taxi with axles, brakes and a fan belt. On a night that has barely dipped below a hundred degrees, the elec-*

*trical power of Tbilisi has been cut again. The moon, however,*

*sheds ample light on our meeting on the cement porch.*

With the tension of a family bereavement coupled with grain alcohol and questions of money, the mood is explosive. Everyone seems to have a different opinion of our obligations and suddenly a month of friendship, of shared meals, of a thousand toasts, of boxing, of laughter, threatens to unravel. Mr Ramiz wisely retreats inside to bed. John, always a touch suspicious of unwarranted kindness, is now convinced that we are being exploited. At the other end of the spectrum lies Ilya.

'These people poor', explains the translator, 'if I have money, I give to them. You want to fuck them? They have money they give it to you, we like brothers. We give them money.'

It is Taran's decision. There is a budget, and it has slowly shrunk. We have already paid Lado rent for our visit, and given money to both him and his brother Baklul for the use of their taxis.

Unfortunately, the raised voices from the initial discussion have attracted a large audience of young men, including Mahir, Lado's boxing son, and several of his friends. There are a lot of fingers being wagged back and forth between the group. We have already agreed to assist with the funeral costs, but with Mr Ramiz still to pay, we are not in a position to surrender the remainder of our budget.

'Perhaps', says Taran, 'the wisest thing would be if everybody went to bed.'

Ilya is in no mood to translate. He waves Taran off and is now conversing in such heated Russian that John finds it impossible to follow. The foreigners retreat. From inside, lying in the darkness, we can hear the arguments dip and rise.

'What do you think's happening?' I ask John.

'Whatever it is,' he says, 'it won't be resolved by a drunken translator.'

Lado comes crashing into our room. 'Money, now. Money, now. Money, now.'

Taran gets up and waves his arms in peace. Arguing in underpants seems to be undermining his influence.

'Ilya,' continues Lado, 'he is hooligan. He is bad man. Very bad man.'

This is hard to fathom. Ten minutes ago, Ilya was arguing in their favour, wanting us to give the remainder of the budget to Lado's household.

'You, I love,' says Lado, pointing at the three of us. 'Ilya . . .' he says, and sends a large gob of spit to the floor between Taran's feet.

Taran walks back out on to the roof and returns with Ilya in hand.

'He was up against the wall,' explains Taran, 'Mahir was waving a fist in his face. He was about to die.'

Ilya, unsurprisingly, is slurring his words. 'They try to fuck you. I help you. They want to fuck you. Fuck them.'

Lado leaves in disgust and we are able to put Ilya to bed.

Electricity returns suddenly to the city and all the lights of the neighbourhood blaze.

Baklul is loitering outside the room.

'Maybe we should pay him a little more for the car,' I suggest, pointing at his shadow. 'Otherwise, it might be hard to sleep.'

'Fine,' says Taran and fishes in his wallet for a few bills and disappears.

I think I can hear Taran being clapped on the back. He returns with an exhausted smile and lies down. It is past two in the morning.

Once more Lado comes bustling into the room. He is now so

drunk he is weaving as if the floor is buckling and subsiding in wooden waves. Taran rises to fend him off. Our director is standing there, half naked, shaking his head and pointing Lado out of the door. 'We just want to sleep,' he explains.

Lado leans in and delivers a large sloppy kiss straight on Taran's mouth. The director wipes it away, and our host disappears into the night. He flicks the light off as he leaves. It has all three of us laughing once more.

The following morning we decide to leave for Azerbaijan even earlier than we intended, just in case there are any repercussions awaiting us from the night before. All past sins between Ilya and Ramiz seem to have been forgiven and they talk quietly in the front seat. Mr Ramiz has developed one new trick to show Ilya. He can now drive along mountain passes while smoking, whistling through the sides of his mouth, and still clutch a hunk of cheese in one hand and a slab of bread in the other.

Our stay in the cities is over. On our return to Baku we will visit northern Azerbaijan, heading into the mountains once more. We will leave Mr Ramiz and his sore lungs behind us, travelling by horse to the top of Mount Shamil, an Avar peak named after the Imam. This is the land of his birth, the land of his rise and fall.

On the way, we are able to discover a little more of what has been happening to the north of us in the past week or two. The information staggers us, if only because, had we been in London or New York, we would have known this news days ago. A company of Islamic rebels crossed the border from Chechnya and invaded Dagestan. They are being led by Shamil Basayev. As usual, there are competing explanations for the latest outbreak of violence. According to the Chechen reports, Basayev only crossed the border because the Russians initiated unprovoked punitive raids into villages with large Muslim populations. Shamil Basayev viewed the mission as an act of support, a move to relieve his Islamic brethren and to deter the Russian aggressors. The Russian press claimed that it was an aggressive push from the breakaway republic in an attempt to create unrest in Dagestan. Basayev's intent, they continued, was to call forth a *jihad* across the Muslim countries of the Caucasus with the hope of creating a pan-Islamic state.

Dagestan's situation was not as simple as Chechnya's. Not only is it a state still fully funded by Russia, but it is also split into over thirty ethnic groups, most with competitive claims. Those rebels who crossed the border found themselves fighting the Russians in isolated pockets, then beating a quick retreat into Chechnya. Regardless of whoever instigated the latest conflict, Moscow had now paused, concentrating her troops on the Dagestani side of the border. It seemed inevitable that a repeat of the 1994 war was about to take place, and in such a climate once again the ghost of Imam Shamil was summoned.

The lines were already being drawn throughout the Caucasus. Though the Chechen positions in Dagestan were many miles from the Georgian border, Russian war planes had 'accidentally' bombed the neighbouring village to Shateli. For two days, the Kremlin denied that the planes had been Russian, then confessed to the mistake and apologized. It was a warning shot across Georgia's bows, a reminder that the country contained Russian military bases and that the road from Shateli between Georgia and Chechnya would be watched, lest support for the rebels be smuggled north.

In the town of Zagatalla, the unofficial capital of Avaria, we wait for our contact, Mr Aziz. Zagatalla sits at the confluence of three rivers. If you turn your back on the few concrete apartment buildings, the rest of the town seems idyllic, quiet tree-lined streets, single-storey cottages, the remnants of a Russian fortress. Behind

Zagatalla are densely wooded foothills; beyond them, cloud-covered peaks. Twice, in 1853 and 1854, Shamil led attacks on the Russian garrison at Zagatalla. Both ended in bloody failure. It is the largest Avar town and may still have the Russian castle ruins, but also a tiny and faintly ridiculous museum dedicated to Shamil. It houses Shamil's bed, odd since he never slept in one, and Shamil's saddle, which he never sat on. Both, it turns out, were merely ill-chosen gifts for the Imam.

We are sitting on a bench in a green garden, dominated by a bronze bust of the most famous Avar son, Shamil. The Imam has an omniscient look about him, as if he knows full well the troubles that lie just to the north. Mr Aziz emerges from a small brick house across the street. He is tall, wiry, quiet but well spoken, rarely blinking. A schoolteacher by trade, I can imagine him smiling before an unruly class, disregarding misbehaviour, content to reach only those who wish to understand.

'What is happening in Dagestan?' we ask.

'Everything', says Aziz, 'is brewing again.'

'Is it safe to go so close?' asks Taran.

'I think so,' says Aziz.

He explains to me how to ride an Avar horse. 'Tch tch,' means go. 'Brrrrrr,' means stop. My riding experience is strictly limited, but still enough to know there is more to it than that. At the first bend in the river, my horse approaches John's and rears. His follows suit.

'Don't you know anything?' shouts John, trying to get his snorting horse back under control.

'It's a horse,' I shout.

'It's a stallion,' he shouts back. 'Five stallions, they don't like each other. Keep it away from mine.'

This is easy, because my horse is now heading backwards down the mountain. With difficulty I turn it around and trail the pack.

After five hours, I ache. The only cheering moment comes when Taran, draped in his cameras, falls from his horse. It may be cruel to laugh, but the man had spent a year on horseback in Siberia. In retribution, the earth on a narrow ridge gives way beneath my feet and down I go, horse and rider, falling twenty yards through the mud. The horse rights himself and I brush myself off. Taran and John look down on me. I try to step upwards, but slip even further down the mountain.

'Slap your horse,' shouts Taran.

'Why?'

'Slap your horse.'

I give the horse a crack across its back and it begins to struggle upward, finally returning to the path. I make it upwards on my hands and knees.

Of all the people to be obsessed with our safety, it is the most unlikely, Ilya, who shows the greatest concern that night. Our first camp is not even five miles from the town of Zagatalla, near a pretty mountain stream, hidden between a pair of thick copses. We light a fire, watch the sun fall, and sit and talk. The darker it gets, the emptier the bottles, the more gloomy Ilya's prognosis becomes.

'We keep watch tonight,' he says. 'This not New York, this Kavkas. There is war to the north.'

We had had guns organized, but had concluded that the mixture of firearms and alcohol was potentially disastrous and had opted to leave without weapons.

'This wolf country,' says Ilya. 'And bear. And Chechen. Just mountain between us and bad men. They come, they tie us like dogs, we live in pits. I do not want this. I want to drink together again.'

'Shut up,' says John. 'Stop trying to spook us.'

'This hot spot,' says Ilya, and his arm sweeps the pitch-black panorama, 'in all the world, this hot spot.'

'If we light a fire,' says Taran, 'we'll only make it easier for them to find us. Just go to bed.'

An hour after we retire, I hear the sound of voices approaching in the little valley beneath us. I nudge Ilya in the tent beside me. We have one knife between us. Slowly and quietly, we unzip the tent. Ilya slithers away. I watch from the dark. Two minutes later, Ilya is waving a torch back up. 'No problem, look.' He shines the light on our visitors. A pimp from the town beneath has marched up a selection of whores. I zip up the tent and attempt to sleep. I dream of Chechens or wolves, who will descend and rid us of the noises that rise from beneath.

The second day, as we ride further up the mountain everybody is scowling at Ilya, who has rarely seemed so content. Moods are restored when the ground levels for half a mile and a perfect glade comes into view. In the middle of this small stretch of long grasses is an enormous bear stool. To the left are a thick knot of blackberry bushes, to the right a parade of plum trees. We dismount and walk from one side to the other, filling our mouths, staining our hands. Finally, we collect wood to use tonight.

At about ten thousand feet, the mountain we have been climbing levels out, then connects to brother mountains to the left and to the right. Beneath us we can see a vast flock of sheep grazing quietly, white wisps close enough to one another to seem like clouds. We head north, the path now no wider than a single horse, the drop to the left harmful to John's vertigo. I notice him staring dead ahead. Clouds dip down to meet us, so thick at times that I cannot see Taran's horse twenty yards in front of me. We can hear dogs barking ahead. As the mist thins, we find ourselves in a graveyard, two miles above the sea. The dogs patrol, charging the horses, then shying away. The stallions snort, but do not panic. Aziz waves us through.

Just before sunset, we stop to camp, but once again the mist has thickened, so it is hard to tell if we have reached the top of the mountain.

'You will see in the morning,' says Aziz. He wanders into the mist, in search of a shepherd. An hour later he returns with dinner, a young lamb draped over his shoulder. For over two months, I have eaten mutton or lamb at least once a day. Sheep fat seems to sweat from my body. Tonight, I cannot even look at it. I walk outside the circle of fire and launch the meat from the mountain heights. A harmless drizzle gathers force and soon the heavy downpour forces us into our tents.

'Goodnight,' says Aziz and points towards the sky. 'Rain is good, it is a welcome from the mountains.'

Ilya is asleep within moments, still exhausted from his previous night's work. I sit, listening to the rain beat against the tent, a torch in my mouth, making notes, accompanied by the snorts of the horses which are tethered in a circle around us.

I write: 'There is no question that mountains, mist, horses and wild dogs lend a Caucasian romance to our final journey, but it is part of the myth, part of the menace. Those who live in the mountains, even those who visit them, cannot help but think of Imam Shamil.' Looking back over my notes, I find the comments of Vahid Mustafayev, the Azeri war reporter. 'I lost my brother because he knew of Shamil,' Vahid had said. I write: 'Too many people think of Shamil as a destructive power, but he was a builder, wanting independence. We think the wrong thing, of Shamil only as warrior.'

In an entry a week later, I find the same idea expressed once more, by the Minister of Foreign Affairs for the Karabagh Republic. She was in complete agreement with the Azerbaijani.

What is happening in the Caucasus now is the direct consequence of Imam Shamil's war. For me, Shamil has become a poetic, and not a political image. You know what one of the Chechen leaders said? He said that the war in the Caucasus would never have been lost if Imam Shamil were a Chechen. Shamil remains a source of romantic inspiration, much of it dangerous.

In my tent, obscured by a night of mist and rains, I imagine that you can see Mount Shamil from miles away. In its shadow grow young men convinced that they are as indefatigable as their ances tors. They are willing to wage war against overwhelming odds. Even today, fighting is still viewed as one of the few honourable occupations in Chechnya. There is no Chechen economy outside the black market, and involvement in such illegal trading necessitates a boldness and aggression that stokes the fires of independence as surely as did the raids of the nineteenth century. Stories are still passed on between generations, so many stories of war that it is natural for young men to grow up wishing to emulate their forefathers. The greater exaggeration that history is retold with, the more pressing the need to emulate it, the more dangerous such acts become. Who, after all, would believe that a country the size of Wales could oppose Russian might, again and again?

Shamil was a reaction to the Russian encroaches. He was not an ideal, his own manner often as cruel and barbaric as the Russians'. While theirs was a greed for dominion, his was essentially a thirst for freedom. Everything was a mirror to the Russian approach: Christianity was combated with Islam, the plains with the mountains, infantry and artillery with guerrilla attacks. The religious extremism that shaped his campaign also ended it. Religious fervour, he was to discover, was an individual's choice and proved inappropriate as a foundation stone to build a nation upon. 'I think', the Minister of Karabagh had concluded, 'that radicalization of any national liberation movement starts to subvert the movement from within. If it is leaning on only the radical elements, it loses the support of the major part of the population, the mass of which is not ready to subscribe to bloodshed and a long war.' It is heart-breaking to think of the process beginning again now just miles to the north, as I fall asleep, under the same clouds, the same rain.

In the morning we are greeted with the most extraordinary sight. The sun has not yet risen. I wake and step out of the tent into the thickest fog, my torch barely marking the ground beneath my feet. I hear the horses neighing, tethered to stakes driven into the ground, communicating with one another in snorts and whin-nies. Mr Aziz is at work on a fire, battling against sodden logs. It is just before six, the sun must be coming. You can feel the heat of its presence further up the mountain and suddenly it arrives, not with the usual signal of light, but by pushing at the fog.

The mists are swept from us like a blanket, one second above our camp, the next below, breaking in an exact line, moving quickly down the mountain so that beneath us now lies a vast ocean of fog. The sun is bright today. I flip off the torch. Everyone has emerged from his tent and moves off to check on his horse. Aziz points down the mountain. The sun is casting our giant shadows against the fog as it hits a neighbouring peak some miles away. Our figures must be half a mile in height. The shadows stand side by side, holding the reins of horses as large as hills. It is like witness-ing the creation of a myth.

# Epilogue

*We left the Caucasus in September 1999. Weeks later, the Russian forces began their second campaign of the decade against Chechnya with familiar bluster. Grozny had become a well-defended sniper's paradise. Every day the citizens of Grozny endured bombing runs by Russian war planes. Those who had remained no longer trusted the humanitarian corridors provided by the Russians, after several attacks on unarmed convoys were reported by the United Nations. Finally, in January 2000, the rebels were driven from Grozny. During the week before the end of the siege, Russian agents had supplied the Chechens with correct information of unguarded escape routes, allowing small groups of rebels to flee the capital. By the time Basayev was ready to move the remainder of his troops out of the city, the information given by the Russian agents was regarded as gospel. The Chechens were directed into a minefield, resulting in over three hundred deaths or casualties, the single greatest loss the*

*Russians had yet inflicted on the rebels. Shamil Basayev lost his*

*foot, a video of the amputation sent by the Chechens to Western*

*agencies to prove that the warlord remained alive.*

In *Hadji Murad* Tolstoy levelled a criticism at Russia. It seems not as apt now as it was six years ago. Tolstoy wrote that what happened in the north Caucausus is

> what always happens when a state, having large-scale military strength, enters into relations with primitive, small peoples, living their own independent life. Under the pretext of self-defence (even though attacks are provoked by the powerful neighbour), or the pretext of civilizing the ways of a savage people (even though the savage people are living a life incomparably better and more peaceable than the civilizers) or else under some other pretext, the servants of large military states commit all sorts of villainy against small peoples, while maintaining that one cannot deal with them otherwise.

The journalist and historian, Anatol Lieven, writing from Chechnya in 1997, balances the perspective. 'Sometimes if a state is weak, it is because society is very strong, too strong to be disciplined by state power. While this can give the appearance of anarchy, it can also provide great underlying strengths, at least in the face of particular challenges – something which is exemplified by Chechnya.'

What seemed to have happened between the end of the war in 1996 and the re-emergence of conflict in 1999 was that this 'appearance of anarchy' was now running more deeply in Chechen society. Basayev's decision to enter Dagestan, even if it was in relief of embattled Muslim communities, was apparently made without permission of the Chechen President, Mashkadov. It brought about a war as ruthless as that endured only four years before.

By 1996, the country was exhausted. Dudayev's death may have secured him a place in the Caucasian pantheon of heroes, but during his time as President of Chechnya not one school was built. The nation had grown tired of war, yet during the brief interval of peace no one had looked to the future. Basayev's provocation of Russia in 1999 frustrated many more people than it pleased. In the winter of 2000, Lieven declared that the true 'tragedy of the Russians' ham-fisted brutality is that they might have attracted the support of most Chechens had they tried to work peacefully with the President to expel extremist groups'. Shamil Basayev best sums up the situation that Russia helped to create. In November of 1999 he explained that though 'we may fight among ourselves, against Russia we will always be as one'. Russia is a temporary focus, but it has never completely prevented the internal cracks from showing.

Heroes of the Caucasus may often look like men who are fighting for freedom, but such a fight necessitates that there is an enemy to combat. In hindsight, it seems as if Russia's original presence in the Caucasus was the safest path to peace. The relationship between Cossacks and lowland Chechens included a fair degree of assimilation from both sides, one that might well have led to a creeping, yet predominantly unhostile, border in Russia's south.

Once General Yermolov had ignited fires of nationalism within the Chechens, and, more importantly, drawn a strict line between Cossack and Chechen, the stage for the ongoing hostilities was set. Chechens tempted by trading in the plains with the Cossacks were driven back into the mountains, to the laws of the Adats. The words of the Decembrist Mikhail Orlov echo teasingly from 1825: 'It is just as hard to subjugate the Chechens and other peoples of this region as to level the Caucasian range. This is something to achieve not with bayonets but with time and enlightenment.'

The irony is that perhaps the weakened state of Russia in the early twenty-first century made it a more dangerous opponent than the ordered Tsarist of Nicholas and Alexander. So strong are Russia's pains of phantom empire that the loss of Chechnya and Dagestan, her buffer zone against the Muslim nations of Turkey and Iran, is now incomprehensible both to the lawmakers and the Russian population. Proving military strength against a land as savaged and exhausted as Chechnya might well have seemed heartless had Chechnya not spent two years proving itself a worthy adversary.

Russia has repeatedly complained that there is no Chechen state to speak of with which to seek out a political compromise, maintaining that this was part of the dilemma of continuing a war against terrorism. Not only had Russia relied on Basayev's attack on Chechnya for boosting support at home, but popular opinion for the invasion was further bolstered by a bombing campaign directed on Russian soil in the summer of 1999. Over three hundred people, mainly women and children, died in these attacks that the Russian Government blamed on Chechen insurgents. Though the *Daily Telegraph* published an article claiming that there was now proof that the bombs were planted by the Russian security forces, no firm conclusion has been reached. What cannot be doubted is that Chechnya had become a political football just before the Russian elections of 2000, and that President-elect Vladimir Putin's hard line against the breakaway republic had rocketed his popularity.

Two months into the last desperate battle for Grozny, the Russian general Kazantsev told Reuters, 'If martial law is introduced, then I will finish this war in a week. I will flatten this place with bombs.' Then, as if remembering his role, 'But that would be war. What I am conducting is a counter-terrorist operation.' Still, his wish would soon be granted.

Once again, the echoes of Chechnya between the mild-nineteenth and turn of the twenty-first century are remarkable. Substituting for the thinned Chechen forests are the modern cities. Trees, brush and undergrowth have been replaced with rows of houses, apartment blocks, courtyards and alleyways every bit as dark and daunting to the modern Russian soldier.

When Chechen fighters were finally driven from the outskirts of Grozny, the Russian military executed the equivalent action of the destruction of Chechnya's forests. Any building large enough to hide a sniper was systematically dynamited. Eric Bouver, a French photographer who travelled through the former city of half a million in April 2000 said, 'I did not find a single building intact.' It is hard to think of any modern equivalent of such complete urban destruction outside of Stalingrad. It was a comparison often made without a trace of irony by Russian commanders in the 1990s.

The Russians also destroyed buildings in the nineteenth century. Robert Chenciner, in his book on Dagestani tradition, estimates that in certain regions, some *aouls* were levelled every three years during the Murid Wars, rebuilt by their inhabitants in the full knowledge that they would fall again.

The individual dynamiting of buildings in the 1990s makes an interesting but not perfect comparison with the felling of trees in the 1850s. Both create open space, leaving nowhere for the enemy to hide. It is impossible, however, to forget the central difference between the forests of Chechnya and concrete Grozny. The trees rose from native soil, while Grozny was built by Russian and Cossack hands as a fortress. The Russian Government has announced that it has no plans to rebuild the city: it is simply too costly an exercise, needing billions of roubles that a government is unlikely to direct towards such a thorny region as Chechnya. It is not the city of Grozny they are interested in, but the territory of Chechnya, still the favoured route of Caspian oil pipelines. If the razed city lies as a symbol of retribution, it is also a monument for the inability of Russians to control the Chechen population: through war, through propaganda, through politics, through deportation. The Chechen identity remains strong, but how strong?

Already, the strength of the Chechen black market has begun to reveal an economic divide that the country has never dealt with before. Perhaps such uneven wealth will begin to splinter the family structures that Chechens have cherished for so long. Either way, the effects of the wars of the 1990s will be hard to distinguish as long as the threat of Russian intervention remains.

Morton Abramowitz, a veteran American envoy, once said that 'diplomats like to export problems to the future'. Chechnya has remained a thorn in Russia's side since the days of Peter the Great. Perhaps, then, it will not just be bloodshed that echoes through the years. Perhaps the lessons learned in the thirty years of war conducted against Imam Shamil will also be drawn into the present. Neither country can change its shared border, no more than Chechnya could level her mountains, or Russia raise her steppes.

In 1859, the treaty signed by Imam Shamil and Prince Bariatinksy declared, on behalf of the Tsar:

1   That the Russian Government allows you forever to adhere to the faith of your forefathers.
2   That you never will be recruited or turned to Cossackship.
3   That appointed authorities will rule by the Sharia,

while justice and prosecution will be executed in public courts, composed of the best people elected by you and appointed by the authorities.

4    That your rights of property will be kept inviolable. Your land estates, both hereditary and apportioned by the Russian authorities, will be allotted to your inherent possession by laws and plans.

It was a compromise in victory that the Russia of the 1990s was not willing to show in defeat. Most of today's political thinking stemming from the West deals with the concerns about Islamic fundamentalism. Yet, certainly in Chechnya, Islam is merely the most cohesive representation of pride and thirst for nationalism, most practised when it can be applied against something, namely Russia. The north Caucasus has given more than enough evidence century after century that it will never truly capitulate. Every announcement of subjugation, every treaty, every headline, has sooner of later been mocked by the flexing of a bellicose people.

# Notes

1. Blanch, Lesley, *Sabres of Paradise,* p.255.
2. Baddeley, John F., *The Russian Conquest of the Caucasus,* p.xxxvi.
3. Solzhenitsyn, Alexander, *The Gulag Archipelago* Vol.3, p.405.
4. Baddeley, op. cit., p.xxxvii.
5. Mackie, J. Milton, *Schamyl and the Circassian War*, p.22.
6. Veliamenov, Commentary, as quoted in Baddeley, op. cit., p.114.
7. Sava, George, *Valley of Forgotten People*, p.7.
8. Baddeley, op. cit., pp.279–80.
9. Mackie, op. cit., p.155.
10. Baddeley, op. cit., p.313.
11. Ibid., p.387.
12. Blanch, op. cit., pp.370–1.
13. Baddeley, op. cit., p.xxxv.
14. Ibid.
15. Dediamenov, as quoted in Baddeley, op. cit., pp.463–4.
16. Baddeley op. cit., pp.xxi–ii.
17. Lieven, Anatol, *Chechnya: Tombstone of Russian Power*, p.55.
18. Van Creveld, Martin, *The Transformation of War*, p.25.
19. Lieven, op. cit., p.123.

# Bibliography and Further Reading

Ahmed, S. Z. – *Twilight on the Caucasus*, A.E.R. Publications, North Carolina, 1997

Allen, W. E. D. and Muratoff, Paul – *Caucasian Battlefields*, Cambridge University Press, Cambridge, 1953

Ascherson, Neil – *Black Sea*, Jonathan Cape, London, 1995

Avtorkhanov, Abdurahman – *The North Caucasus Barrier*, St Martin's Press, New York, 1992

Baddeley, John F. – *The Russian Conquest of the Caucasus*, Longman, London, 1908

Baddeley, John F. – *The Rugged Flanks of Caucasus*, Oxford University Press, Oxford, 1940

Baldwin, Oliver – *The Questing Beast*, Grayson and Grayson, London, 1935

Bitov, Andrei, *A Captive of the Caucasus*, Farrar Strauss Giroux, New York, 1992

Blanch, Lesley – *Sabres of Paradise*, Carroll and Graf, New York, 1995

Brzezinski, Zbigniew – *The Grand Chessboard*, Basic Books, New York, 1997

Chenciner, Robert – *Daghestan: Tradition and Survival*, St Martin's Press, New York, 1997

Drancy, Anna – *Souvenirs d'une Francaise, Captive de Shamyl*, Paris, 1860

Dumas, Alexandre – *Adventures in Caucasia*, Chilton Books, New York, 1962

Dunlop, John B. – *Russia Confronts Chechnya*, Cambridge University Press, Cambridge, 1998

Edwards, H. Sutherland – *Captivity of Two Russian Princesses in the Caucasus*, London, 1857

Eliot, Mark – *Azerbaijan with Georgia*, Trailblazer, West Sussex, 1999

Foster, Ruth – *The Stone Horsemen*, Howard W. Sams, New York, 1965

Gall, Carlotta – *Chechnya: Calamity in the Caucasus*, NYU Press, New York, 1998

Gammar, Moshe – *Russian Strategies in the Conquest of Chechnia and Daghestan 1825–1859* (article), New York, 1992

Gammar, Moshe – *Muslim Resistance to the Tsar: Shamil and the Conquest of Chechnya and Dagestan*, Frank Cass, London, 1994

Gamzatov, Rasul – *My Daghestan*, Progress Publishers, Moscow, 1970

Goltz, Thomas – *Azerbaijan Diary*, M. E. Sharpe, New York, 1999

Hamid, Muhammad – *Imam Shamil: The first Muslim guerilla leader*, Adam Publishers, Delhi, 1991

Hildinger, Erik – *Warriors of the Steppe*, Sarpedon Books, New York, 1997

Hopkirk, Peter – *The Great Game*, Oxford University Press, Oxford, 1990

Karny, Yo'av – *Highlanders: A Journey to the Caucasus*, Farrar Strauss Giroux, New York, 2000

Keegan, John – *A History of Warfare*, Vintage Books, New York, 1994

Lang, David Marshall – *Armenians: A People in Exile*, Unwin, London, 1988

Layton, Susan – *Russian Literature and Empire*, Cambridge University Press, Cambridge, 1994

Lermontov, Mikhail – *A Hero of Our Time*, Knopf, New York, 1958

Lieven, Anatol – *Chechnya: Tombstone of Russian Power*, Yale University Press, New Haven, 1998

Mackie, J. Milton – *Life of Schamyl*, J. P. Jewett and Co., Boston, 1856

Mackie, J. Milton – *Schamyl and the Circassian War*, John P. Jewett and Co., Boston, 1856

Maclean, Fitzroy – *To Caucasus*, Little, Brown and Co., Boston, 1976

Marsden, Philip – *The Crossing Place*, Flamingo, London, 1994

Marsden, Philip – *The Spirit Wrestlers and Other Survivors of the Russian Century*, Flamingo, London, 1998

Maude, Aylmer – *Leo Tolstoy*, Dodd, Mead and Co., London, 1918

Redgate, A. E. – *The Armenians*, Blackwell, London, 1998

Remnick, David – *Resurrection*, Vintage, New York, 1998

Rustaveli, Shota – *The Knight in Panther's Skin*, Tbilisi, 1968

Sava, George – *Valley of Forgotten People*, Faber and Faber, London, 1941

Severin, Tim – *The Jason Voyage*, Hutchinson and Co., London, 1985

Smith, Sebastian – *Allah's Mountains*, I. B. Tauris and Co., London, 1998

Solzhenitsyn, Alexander – *The Gulag Archipelago*, Harper and Row, New York, 1992

Suny, Ronald Grigor – *The Making of the Georgian Nation*, Indiana University Press, Bloomington, 1994

Ternon, Yves – *The Armenians: History of a Genocide*, Caravan Books, New York, 1981

Tolstoy, Leo – *Prisoner of the Caucasus*, Oxford University Press, Oxford, 1917

Tolstoy, Leo – *Hadji Murad*, Orchises Press, Virginia, 1996

Tolstoy, Leo – *The Cossacks*, Everyman's Library, New York, 1994

Van Creveld, Martin – *The Transformation of War*, The Free Press, New York, 1991

Van der Leeuw, Charles – *Storm over the Caucasus*, Curzon, Richmond, 1999

Walker, Christopher J. – *Visions of Ararat*, I. B. Tauris and Co., London, 1997

Wells, J. G. – *The Complete History of the Russian War*, J. G. Wells, New York, 1856

Wilson, A. N. – *Tolstoy*, Ballantine Books, New York, 1988

# Index